PRAISE FOR *HE'S JUST NOT THAT INTO YOU*

"No ego-soothing platitudes. No pop psychology. No cute relationship tricks. He's just not that into you."

—Washington Post

"Brims with straight talk about the boy-meets-girl game, delivered with hefty doses of humor from the Y chromosome's mouth."

—USA Today

"A surprisingly fascinating addition to the cultural canon of single, urban life."

—Los Angeles Times

"Evil genius."

—New York Times

PRAISE FOR *IT'S CALLED A BREAKUP BECAUSE IT'S BROKEN*

"You will get through this, and you'll do it faster with the help of *It's Called a Breakup Because It's Broken.*"

—Glamour

"Behrendt's frankness—never too harsh—is as winning as ever."
—Publishers Weekly

"Insightful, been-there-have-the-scars-to-prove-it wisdom."
—New York Post

Diversion Books
A Division of Diversion Publishing Corp.
443 Park Avenue South, Suite 1004
New York, New York 10016
www.DiversionBooks.com

For more information, email info@diversionbooks.com

First Diversion Books edition July 2013.

Print ISBN: 978-1-62681-120-1
eBook ISBN: 978-1-626811-07-2

IT'S JUST A F***ING DATE

SOME SORT OF BOOK ABOUT DATING

GREG BEHRENDT
& AMIIRA RUOTOLA

DIVERSIONBOOKS

CONTENTS

WE DIDN'T THINK WE HAD TO DO THIS

The book you hold in your hands or are reading on your phone, shoe, holographic portal or other technology breakthrough reading device that used to be called a book wasn't originally written for you. It was conceived for territories like the UK and Australia where people are more likely to go the pub, have a pint then wind up with a couple of kids. We don't need to worry about the Americans! We know that because they're reading our other books. They're breaking up with guys that aren't that into them and learning that a breakup means a relationship is broken and not fixable. There's this new superhuman race of empowered relationship ninjas that drink green juices, go to Soul Cycle and Cardio Barre and don't settle for anything less than a guy that meets the standards they set for themselves. We can retire from writing relationship books and go raise our girls in the new utopian world of healthy relationships ... *or so we thought.* Along comes a more robust Internet, reality television that devalues the human relationship, apps to upload your every thought, birds to slingshot across your phone, electronic dance music, and suddenly we are a compromised people. Too lazy to date, too busy tweeting to actually meet people, too self-obsessed to squeeze another person into our "selfie," yet requiring little more than a thumbs up "like" or emoji flirtation to assume a connection with another human being. Relegating our self-esteem to our social networking status rather than actual human contact. "ENOUGH!" we shouted from our old people chairs. This won't do! We have daughters who will someday "date," and we'd like there to be dating when they do; otherwise, they are in for many nights at home playing celebrity with their sad, but always well-dressed, parents. Look, we are not against technology, in fact quite the opposite! We love that there are more ways for people to meet than ever but there's a difference between your relationship with your *best* friends and with your accumulated (using the term loosely) "friends," "tweeps," "likers" and "followers." Your best friends know you, love you and support you. Your "friends," "tweeps," "likers," and "followers" know what your morning coffee foam art or sleeping dog looks like. Can you see the difference? There's "knows you" and then there's "KNOWS" you. The same should go for the people you decide to enter into any kind of romantic or sexual relationship with. That's why we've decided to put out *It's Just a F***ing Date!* Because even though we know you're smart enough to know better, you still do dumb things. And by the way, you're the only one. The rest of us are perfect. With that in mind, know that we have your best interest at heart and want you gorgeous natives of the electronic age to get the most out of your life by attracting QUALITY people, not just QUANTITY. You know how everything old is new again, like moustaches, Pabst Blue Ribbon and banjos? Hey, Coachella generation, why not embrace dating? Make that the new old thing that's cool again!

A CALL TO THE
WINNER DATER WITHIN

So your dating life is in the crapper and you've just about given up on the idea altogether at this point. And seriously, what's with guys, right? Why don't they ask women out? Why does it have to be so damn hard to date? Or what ever happened to dating, for that matter? Used to be that a guy would have the sack to ask a girl out. Then he'd pick her up at her house and take her out for dinner, a movie, or a cup of coffee and some conversation. Then both parties would decide if they wanted to do it again next week. There was protocol. A courtship. A standard set of guidelines to follow for this age-old ritual outlined by our "Foredaters." Now who even knows what dating is?

WHAT IS A DATE?

If you hook up at a bar and go home together, are you dating? If he text messages you, "What are you wearing?" are you dating? If he tells you where he's going with his friends after work and tells you to bring your friends, are you dating? If he changes his status on his homepage to "it's complicated," are you dating? If he sends you an emoji of a smiling pig, are you dating? If he uploads a photo of your shoes, are you dating? It's not cut and dry any more; in fact, it's become completely absurd. Sadly, dating has become somewhat obsolete, having been edged out of the lineup by hooking up, hanging out, texting pictures of your boobs or penis, and random sex. Why is that? Because both men and women have said by their actions and willingness that they don't need the formality of a date to give their time, the privilege of their company or even their bodies. We've become a world of non-daters, and judging from the masses of unsatisfied singles that we hear from and about, we'd surmise that the whole non-dating thing's not going that great. It's too confusing, too casual, too grey and not enough black and white. Courtship has gone so far astray that it's come down to proximity and laziness. Like if you stand next to someone long enough at a concert then eventually you'll pair up and be in a relationship with them without any actual effort, action or decision having been put into it.

BACK TO BASICS

It's time for a change and aside from non-dating, the only other option to dating would be arranged marriages or marriage by lottery system. So it seems like now's the time to figure out how to date again because you may not like ending up with #4 8 15 16 23 42. You obviously like yourself enough to pick up this book and consider the idea of improving your dating or non-dating life, and for that we love you. Hooray, we just hugged! Now having said that, we will not coddle you. This is not a touchy-feely "you're great so everyone should think you're great" book. This is a "how bad do you want it and to what lengths will you go to achieve what you truly deserve and then be willing to throw it all away because after all It's Just a F***ing Date!" kind of book. We have made our living being straight with you about our experiences and we've done it wrong ourselves enough times. But ONLY after you've done it wrong so many times will you have that moment of awakening, of clarity, where you admit, "*I do it wrong. I need to do it differently.*"

By reading this book you are entering a no bullshit area. Unlike some of your friends, we will not sign off on your questionable behavior and will continually demand better of you. We will not buy the rationalizing that you do to make it okay nor the excuses you make for yourself or someone else who's giving you less than you deserve. Now is the time to redefine what kind of dater you are and how you date. So buckle up ladies because you've come to the right place. You know what we've got? We've got answers and we've got plans for you

REALITY CHECK!

The reality of dating is that almost every date you go on is not going to work out or turn into a lasting and meaningful relationship. In fact, every date and relationship won't work out until you find the one that does. That's how it works. That's how life works and dating works. There are no shortcuts or loopholes and absolutely everyone is in the same boat as you. The only difference is how you approach these dates and the attitude you have when you get there. You can continue to dread them, be annoyed by the whole process, have expectations that are sure to disappoint you and project the futility you feel about the whole thing. OR you can let go of all of it, tell yourself that *It's Just a F***ing Date!* and not the rest of your life; that it probably won't work out in the long run but might be fun nonetheless. With those expectations you'll have a much better time than you thought you would. Because *that* actually is the point of dating: an opportunity to spend time one-on-one to see if there's a spark. That's it. Dating was never meant to be a tortuous obstacle course that you had to suffer through, nor the culmination of all our dreams that aren't being fulfilled crashing down again when it doesn't work out. And if that's what dating is for you, you've got to ask yourself what's with the self-emotional terrorism and why are you doing that to yourself? Then you have to tell yourself to knock it the f*** off. YOU CONTROL HOW YOU DATE, NOT ANYONE ELSE, INCLUDING THE PERSON YOU'RE ON THE DATE WITH. So let go of the old dating patterns that aren't working for you; embrace the ideals of dating like a winner and being the best you that you can be.

MY NAME IS AMIIRA AND I'M A BAD DATER

It seems like I should have figured that I was doing it wrong after the fiasco of my first marriage. Want to talk about going fast? It was love at first sight ... except for the fact that he had a girlfriend. It was a matter of months before they broke up and we got together, so to make up for lost time we spontaneously got married in Vegas by an Elvis impersonator. That's good, right? I had never been to his home, we hadn't met each other's families and probably didn't know each other's middle names. We did have similar record collections, so that should have been enough. Well, not surprisingly, it turns out that we didn't really know each other that well, along with other biggies that eluded us, like similar values and the desire for children. So that didn't work out, but I learned my lesson about jumping in too fast. Or did I? My next relationship went straight from "Nice to meet you" to "We should go to Barbados on vacation." At least I had seen his house before packing my bikinis, plus we did have similar record collections. But ultimately we got too intense too quickly and we burned out on each other. Strike two! It'd be nice if there wasn't a strike three, but there he was and who could resist the best friend that proclaims his love after too many Heinekens? Not I. So into instant boyfriend I fell. You know what happens when you go from being best friends to instant significant others? You realize that you probably weren't meant to be boyfriend/girlfriend but are trapped in a relationship with a person you love but "not in that way." That didn't end well. So at this point I recognized that speed was my foe and the way I dated wasn't working for me. The relationships I got myself into were plagued by the lack of certainty from rushing myself or someone else into feelings that weren't fully cultivated. Then I met Greg Behrendt, who must have been doing the same thing in his life, because he was Mister Take It Slow. Nice. We went out on our first date, which was very good; in fact, we decided that we would go out again while still on the date. But then I broke up with him. Huh? It's a long story involving an ex-boyfriend that wouldn't go away. However, he said the most amazing thing upon hearing my true but cockamamie-sounding story about the ex-boyfriend on my lawn that prohibited me from dating him right now. He said, "It's also okay if you don't like me like that." What?! Who the hell was this completely self-possessed guy? I told him truly that I didn't know yet whether I liked him but would be interested in finding out. So we dated, the old-fashioned way. He called ahead, asked me out, plans were made and we went on dates. We also dated other people while dating each other. There was no hopping in the sack, no racing to lock it down, no panic about what the other was thinking, feeling, doing. Then one day he said something mind-blowing: "I'm not going to date other people. I only want to go out with you, but I don't expect you to do the same until you're ready to." What?! Who the hell is this guy who is going to stop dating other people but not demand I do the same? I had never even heard something remotely similar to that sentiment. So we continued dating and soon after I came to the same conclusion that he did ... I didn't want to date other people. So there we were as boyfriend and girlfriend because we both truly wanted to be that and had figured it out at our own pace. Revolutionary! Then shortly thereafter he says those three magic words: "I Love You ..." This was followed by the even more magical words that I had never heard before: "... But you don't have to say it back. You don't have to be at the same place emotionally that I am, but I know that I love you and I wanted you to know it." Holy crap!! Are you f***ing kidding me? Who says that? Where did this alien creature come from that is so comfortable in his own feelings that he can allow me to have my own feelings without any pressure, pouting, or weird relationship-ending vibe? That's how foreign the idea of taking things slow and actually figuring your feelings organically was to me. Normally at this point in a relationship I would have felt obligated to blurt it right back and hope that I grew into the feelings later, but because he was so self-possessed it made it effortless for me to be too. That being said, when I actually experienced having a relationship in real time, on my time, it became the one that has lasted the longest and burns the brightest because it's real and taking place in actual time. We're on this journey together side by side instead of one dragging the other behind. Our story is the reason that we decided to write this book, because we know what is possible if you learn to do it right.

THE GOOD, THE BAD & THE SKILLET, OR WHY I TRIED DATING, BY GREG

The decision to start dating was a simple one. It started with a skillet. Not even a nice one, but one of those gunmetal grey, now singed black, workhorse skillets that you burn fried eggs with. "Wait, Greg, are you telling me, the interested reader, that a dirty skillet got you dating? I'm not convinced." Yes, I remember thinking as the greasy black pan was heading towards my skull, "This might not be the right relationship. I'm not choosing the right lady for me." Here's what happened. I was newly "drinks free" (I like that better than sober because it almost sounds like free drinks and that makes people happy) and had been set up with a girl who was also "drinks free." She was foxy and funny with a little edge. Anyway, we went on two dates, one a formal dinner and on the other we hung out at a thing, then had awkward sex too soon and became girlfriend-boyfriend. We didn't really know each other but because we had had sex we felt beholden to one another, and after all, this is how most of my relationships started in the past. Why should this be any different? Ever since college the recipe had been the same. Meet someone, take them out twice, have sex on the third date, become a couple, then fight until done. Ding! It wasn't either person's fault; it was how the game had been set up. I had a pattern, it didn't work and I was sticking to it … until the skillet. I remember calling my mom that day and saying, "… You know what? Maybe I don't end up with anybody. Maybe I'm just destined to be a bachelor. And if that is the case then I'm gonna bachelor the shit out of it." I went at it like a sporting event. I got my own apartment. Taught myself how to cook and to clean. Picked out my own furniture. I went to movies by myself, ate at restaurants by myself and bought my own clothes. I began to teach myself to live as though I might never meet someone, but if I did they'd be blown away by how self-sufficient I was and by my matching bamboo end tables. Like *Field of Dreams*, if you build it they will come. And then the weirdest thing happened: I started meeting girls. Everywhere.

Department stores, flower shops, cafés, softball games and hair salons. See a pattern, fellas? Go to where the girls are. But don't go just to go. The fact that I was now not actively looking for a relationship made me appear to just appear. And for the first time in my life I had the opportunity to date more than one person. And I took it. I'd never done that, so why now? Well, I was at my parents' over a Thanksgiving break, and I was in my mom's office looking for something when I came across an old datebook of hers from when she was dating my dad. I flipped through it and I noticed something almost revolutionary. She had begun dating my dad in May. I know this because his name appears periodically throughout the month. Thursday: Richard. Saturday: Richard. But there are also two other names that appear throughout the month. Steve and Aaron. But as we get to June, Aaron drops off like a stone and Steve's name appears less and less until it fully goes away in July. My dad kicked some dating ass, but the real lesson was my mom wasn't limiting her options until she was sure. I asked her if my dad knew about the other guys. "Not at first. But you didn't ask in those days. It was just assumed that you were dating."

"Assumed you were dating? And he was cool with that?"

"He didn't love it, but he respected it, and in some ways I think it made getting me all the sweeter." Dating?! What a great f***ing idea. Imagine, just going out with someone a few times to see how you really feel about them. So I decided to give it a try. And I found that I liked it and that I was pretty good at it. Were all the dates good? Hell no! There were some nightmares you will read about later on in the book. Did I get my heart broken? Not as badly as if I had tried to turn them into relationships. But it led to the best relationship I ever had with another person on this planet. And that's why I wanted to write this book. There is an option out there, and it's the only one we have besides arranged marriages. Wait, we don't have arranged marriages. But I have supplied a petition at the back of the book if you want to lobby for arranged marriages. So why go on one? Because they work, because dating is the best way to get to know someone you don't know and someone you do, because it's a great way to set the tone and speed for a relationship, because there are snacks, because you might make a friend or meet a future business partner, because you might have the worst night of your life and that could lead to you writing the next great American novel, because you'll never know if you don't because it's just a f***ing date.

WHERE WOMEN BLOW IT, BY AMIIRA

Women always have and always will continue to date a man's potential instead of his reality. We can't help ourselves. It's in a woman's nature to be hopeful and to see the possibilities, the greatness that people possess. Hooray for us; aren't we lovely. We are, but dating someone's potential is probably the biggest mistake women make in relationships and certainly the one that leads to our romantic downfall. That's because there are three types of men: the ones that find our faith in their potential to be appealing, the ones that find our faith in their potential to be a burden ... and the ones that find it appealing at first, then are crushed by the burden of their unreached potential and resentful of the woman they once adored for that very faith.

The problem is that we don't know which of the three the man of our dreams is going to be until it's often too late. Once you've *unintentionally* crushed a man's ego (read: once he decides that he doesn't want to reach the potential *you* have for him) it's hard for him to be excited about you any more. Then it's just a matter of time before the sex starts diminishing, there's bickering where there wasn't any before and the distance between you begins an expansion that is unwieldy.

More often than not, dating a man's potential is the long road to disaster, so listen to who he says he is and take him at his word. If you can love who he is now and not have your attraction be based on who he might become, then you're in good shape. If you're not, well then you best keep looking because most people have different aspirations than you might have for them.

Love isn't swimming upstream.

PART ONE

PREPARE YOURSELF
FOR DATING EXCELLENCE

WARNING!

You are now entering a new way of dating and living. Old habits are not welcome and failure is not an option. Those not willing to make some serious changes should turn back now and get a few cats to keep you company.

THE PRINCIPLE PRINCIPLES OF DATING FOR WINNERS

You were probably skulking around the eBookstore mumbling to yourself: "My dating life's a mess. I sure wish I had some guidelines for dating more successfully." Well today's your lucky day, so buck up, sugarpot, because that's exactly what we have for you! Super Extraordinary Guidelines for Ultra-Successful Winner Dating ™. Dating has become a confusing mess for most single folks out in the world, and quite honestly, it shouldn't be. Dating was one of the most well-structured, well-thought-out things that our generation inherited. How we managed to f*** that one up is a mystery. In our natural evolution as humans and as we've become a more liberal society, we've rid ourselves of ideas or thought processes that don't work, like no premarital sex, the inability of women to vote, etc. ... Certainly there are formalities and expected behaviors that do need updating and revising to keep up with the contemporary times, but dating, as it turns out, may not have been one that needed much. The radical revision of dating that followed the sexual revolution and its continual morphing that has come with the advances in communication technology and social networking has turned dating into a blur of booty calls, ambiguous hanging out and "window-shopping" your Facebook photos, then making assumptions about who someone is rather than getting to know them. And the result is a lot of unhappy and unclear people that are in complete disharmony with their romantic universe.

What women are craving is the clarity that the formality of dating would provide for them. Think about the collective sigh of relief from just the knowledge alone that when you're asked out that you're actually on a date instead of spending the entire time trying to figure out if you're on a date, just hanging out as friends or being sized up as a candidate for casual sex. **DATING IS SOMETHING THAT *YOU* HAVE CONTROL OVER**, so if you want it to change, if you want to take control of your dating life, you have to take it upon yourself to be very serious about and completely committed to HOW you date. You have to have a set of standards that you live and date by *without* exception. Which means FORMULATING A DATING STRATEGY and INSTITUTING DATING POLICY for yourself, then sticking to it. It sounds ridiculous but it's not. In fact, had you done it earlier you might be in a very different place with your love life and been able to save that $4.99 (or whatever this book costs) you spent on this fantastic piece of literature, put it into a high-yielding mutual fund and turned it into at least a billion dollars by the time you retire. (These numbers are guesstimations made by two book writers that have no experience or financial expertise and cannot be held accountable for the way you spend your money.)

We know the word strategy in relation to dating can sound like an underhanded manipulation of another person, and that is NOT at all what we're talking about. **Strategy**, in the dictionary, is defined as: **1.** The science or art of planning or conducting a war or military campaign. (Nope!) **2.** Carefully devised plan of action to achieve a goal or the art of developing or carrying out such a plan. (Wrong again!) **3. An evolutionary theory, a behavior structure, or other adaptation that *improves viability*.** (AHA! Bingo! Now we're talking!)

There's an element of strategy in everything that we do in life, and there's nothing wrong with that. There are choices, actions and consequences. That's what everything in life is and dating is no exception. Like the time you agreed to let the drummer for "Mighty Lemon Phillipshead" come up for a nightcap—*that's a choice*. Then you woke up the next morning to find him in your roommate's bed—*that's a consequence*. To be fair, it was dark in your apartment but still ... No, no, no, that's just another excuse you make to cover for making bad choices. The truth is you actually liked him and hoped to go out on a second date and *had you said goodnight at the front door you might've had a chance*. So let's embrace the idea of creating a strategy for dating and your life so that the choices you make are better. As they say in that popular book that features that guy Jesus, "Faith without works is dead." Meaning **you can believe you want a better dating life but unless you're willing to do the work, nothing will change.** "Wow, you got all serious on me. I didn't think Jesus went on dates." Well now you know why people got so mad about *The DaVinci Code*. But let's get back to you …

If your experiences are anything like the throngs of emails and letters we get complaining about the state of dating, then you know that for most men you encounter, dating is something they only *have* to do if they can't get away with hanging out under less formal circumstances (or they can't get you to fool around with them at the bar). It's probably the single most frustrating thing we hear about in all of our varied "what's the deal with men?" conversations. The deal is that *THEY FOLLOW YOUR LEAD*. That means if you give them the easy way out, they'll take it.

It's important to recognize that while you can change the way a man dresses, you can't change the way he approaches dating. You can only inspire him to want to change that for himself so that he gets to spend time with you. *THE THING YOU DETERMINE IS THE VALUE OF YOUR TIME, THE VALUE OF YOUR COMPANY AND HOW YOU DATE.* Those are the *only* things you are in complete control of, but that's enough to turn the tide. Think about it … **IT'S ONLY WHEN YOU SET THE VALUE OF YOUR TIME LOW AND YOU AGREE TO NON-DATES THAT THEY CAN EXIST FOR YOU.** However, if you maintain a high standard for how you date and you don't accept the premise of quasi dating, non-dating and hanging out, then you leave him with only two choices: to ask you out on a proper date or to do without your company. And if he chooses the latter then you're better off anyway, because getting to spend time with you is a gigantic prize, and that guy only wanted to have sex with you because you're hot.

People need to start Dating again and not participate in Non-Dating if they want to find a real relationship rather than someone to have confusing sex with. "But how do I date amongst all the confusing confusion of dating?" We're glad you asked, because there is a definite right and wrong way to date, and if you want to get good results you have to start dating smarter and better. There's a reason why you're not having success: it's because what you're doing isn't working for you. It's time to change up your game. "But I don't like playing games. Dating shouldn't be about game playing." Yeah, yeah ... We've heard it. The reality is that there is a game to be played when dating and it's called *RESTRAINT*. Quite frankly, when you *reject* that idea, you yourself are playing your own game. It's a game of refusing to look at human nature and the things you already know about friendships, work, eating and every other thing in life, where you take the time to responsibly think to yourself: "I need to do this right. There's an order in which everything happens. If I mess with the order the whole thing will fall apart." Why would you single out dating as the place to say, "Ah, f*** the order! I'm not going in order. I'm going to just tell them now that I love them, blow them in the bathroom or whatever impulsive thing that you know you shouldn't do, because that will either make him want to be with me more or bail, *but at least I'll know now!*" It makes no sense. You don't walk into a job interview and ask where your desk is. You don't make a new friend then, after week one, tattoo their name on your neck. You don't eat shitty all week and wonder why your pants don't fit. Do you see where we're going with this? There's an order to things and dating is no exception.

So what we've devised is a set of guidelines, or rather Super Extraordinary Guidelines for Ultra-Successful Winner Dating ™. These are the key to turning your dating life around and setting the new standard for HOW you date. Like we stated earlier, **you get to determine** the value of your time, the value of your company and most importantly how you date and how you absolutely *DO NOT* date. Grab a fork and dig in, sister, because you've got some dating to do!

Here's a preview of what dazzling principles you're going to have drilled into that pretty little head of yours.

THE 8 SUPER EXTRAORDINARY PRINCIPLES FOR ULTRA-SUCCESSFUL WINNER DATING™

Like yourself and know you're worthy

Start with giving your thighs a break. Why can't you just like them for once after all these years they've supported you?

Get a life, have a life ...

... and don't throw it away when every Tom, Dick and Agnes comes along.

Pretty is as pretty does

Get real about what you're putting out into the world.

Don't accept less than an actual date

Seriously. Stop hooking up with bozos when you're drunk.

Don't freak people out with your need

Crazy + Sexy doesn't always = Cool

Doormats finish last and end up in the dirt

Having some standards and ditching the deal breakers

Don't show the movie before the trailer

Making sex an event, not a given

Not every date is going to turn into a relationship

And a worthwhile one is a marathon, not a sprint

HERE'S THE DEAL

It's Just a F***ing Date! It's a philosophy and an attitude all rolled up into one great big package. It's the difference between expecting something to happen and being surprised when it does. It's letting go of the whole process but not letting go of you. There are things in life you can change—your weight, your appearance, your mindset, etc.—but there is one thing you cannot change and that is *other people*. Try as we might we cannot get people to love us. Even when we are the coolest best version of ourselves someone is going to say, "Not for me." But if we feel good about ourselves we can shrug it off and say, "It's just a f***ing date," and know that there will be others.

When you really want something and you're doing everything you can to make it happen and it's not coming to fruition you have to **let go of the result and do the work anyway**. You can't live inside of a result because it will always disappoint. But if you work towards the goal and *let go* of the result then you'll not only get what you wanted, but will probably get something that's better and different than how you had imagined it. That's how life works. Life comes in a different package than you expect it to. The same goes for dating. You need to show up and see what happens. Well now, that doesn't sound so hard but in fact it is.

This book is going to demand two things from you that may seem to conflict. We are going to ask that you be vigilant in your attempts to better yourself AND not take dating so damn seriously. "So does that mean I have to get all dressed up and try even if I'm not supposed to care about what happens?" Exactly. And you'll be a better person for it.

So pull it together, woman, and let's get ready to date!

What follows is a series of words, punctuation, ideas, ink, paper and pages that you will turn from right to left. In these pages you will get information about how to have a healthy dating life through a process referred to commonly as reading. Now go get 'em!

THE 8 SUPER EXTRAORDINARY PRINCIPLES FOR ULTRA-SUCCESSFUL WINNER DATING™

PRINCIPLE #1
LIKE YOURSELF AND KNOW YOU'RE WORTHY

Find Your Inner Cheerleader, Rock Star, Physicist and Some Self-Esteem

Recently, this woman in her mid-twenties came to us because she was having terrible luck dating. She hadn't had a boyfriend or decent date since high school and couldn't get arrested by a single dude, much less get one to ask her out and pay for dinner. She was cute, had a good personality, and definitely had some sex appeal, but it was as if she had actually been deflated. Her whole energy was sad and dejected. She said, "If I had known that high school was going to be the best it was going to get for me, I would have enjoyed it more or nailed down a guy for the future." She really thought it was over for her at the age of twenty-six. We asked her: What was different in high school? Why did she think she peaked romantically then? She thought about it and responded that she had been a cheerleader in high school. She was happy, popular with a lot of different social groups, was lusted after by teenage boys, celebrated by the football team, got special privileges during school to do cheerleader things like decorate the jocks' lockers, prepare for pep rallies and whatnot, and she was in the spotlight performing at halftime, getting to wear her uniform to school on game days, etc. ... It was an idyllic high school existence, and now she no longer even felt like the same person and certainly wasn't living the same kind of life.

We thought about what she was telling us, what we know

of cheerleaders, and it instantly became clear to us. Cheerleaders are sexy and confident, they're kind of hot shit around the halls of high school and they carry themselves like they're hot shit. Now she was wearing a frumpy outfit that was the antithesis of confident cheerleader, which she told us was how she dressed every day. When we asked her, "Why are you hiding that cheerleader?" it all came pouring out, tears streaming down her face. She admitted that she had put on some weight since high school, she didn't like her body, she had been dumped hard her freshman year of college by not even a good guy but a totally shitty one, and she didn't even feel like herself any more. The truth is she didn't like herself or feel at all worthy of having good things in her life. She didn't feel those great things about herself that she did back in high school, so she didn't carry herself out in the world with the same self-confidence or self-worth. Basically, her self-esteem was completely shot. This girl needed to find her inner Cheerleader; she needed to find her confidence again. And as bad as we felt for her, it was a story we have heard countless times from women of every age, and we had to bring down the hammer. This is the gist of what we told Boohoo Jane the sad Cheerleader ...

Happiness is hard work. It always has been since the beginning of time. It takes diligence to continually set yourself up to win—not competitively but personally—and winning is the kindling for the brightly burning fire of self-esteem and happiness. When your self-esteem is heightened you carry yourself with more assurance, your energy is more vibrant, people respond to you more positively and you are more magnetic, so you attract opportunity. Basically, you walk differently, talk differently, rock differently and in the words of the late, great Justin Timberlake, you're bringing sexy back. (To the best of our knowledge Justin Timberlake is very much alive, but we just wanted to see if you were paying attention.) When your self-esteem is lessened you feel bad about yourself, so you avoid things and people, your energy is heavy and sad, people are less likely to respond to you well, and you repel opportunity (including prospective dates!). If you like yourself, if you love yourself, if you feel good about yourself, if you value yourself, you will feel worthy of good things and you will get good things (like a rockin' boyfriend).

The whole concept of winning on a personal level is simple but not necessarily easy to do. The key is to *constantly* put yourself in a position to feel great about you and keep yourself out of harm's way. This translates into stopping your bad behavior, staying away from the people that provoke your bad behavior, or people that make you feel anything less than good about yourself. Otherwise, your self-esteem pays the price. Being a winner in life means finding a way to keep yourself in the personal space where you're being the best and most vibrant you instead of the smallest you. That is the secret to success in anything you want to do in life. That means not comparing yourself to anyone else and concentrating on you. Because when your self-esteem is in the shitter and you don't feel worthy, you look to others for validation, you settle for crappy things and all you get is crappy things and who wants that?

Let's break it down for a moment before we sum it up in a fancy gold-plated nutshell with rims for you. (For those of you who haven't seen any hip-hop videos lately, "rims" are like jewelry for your car wheels—the fancy flashy bits in the middle of the tire that often spin counterclockwise or blind you with their shine and ornamentation.) You started out with so much promise, with endless possibilities for what you can do with your life and who you can become. From the moment you come out of the womb, you have the potential to be anything from Mayor McCheese to running the Free World, who knows?! (By the way, the McCheese gig pays better and is much less stressful, but damn is it hot in that hamburger suit.) From early on we are encouraged, applauded even, for our first accomplishments, be it learning to walk, saying our first words, actually making it into our mouth with the spoonful of bananas instead of down our front. The ovation continues for you lucky ones who grow up surrounded by people who love and support you and whose greatest joy is to build you up after every foul ball, good try, or embarrassing failure. *The great promise that we're talking about is simply the existence of self-esteem.* When you're older you can find it for yourself, but for many it is what you are given, brick by brick, every time you are told that you are good, the world is your oyster, you can do anything you put your mind to, or you're much prettier than your cousin Jenna. (What a sea hag she is.)

So you have this self-esteem, this self-worth all stored up, but then at various points along your journey to here you've lost some of the value you once had for yourself because that's part of the experience of this life. That's the rub. We all have events that reduce our self-esteem and disappointments that make us question our worth, be it socially, academically, professionally or romantically. It only takes getting your heart smashed when your boyfriend dumps you for a younger girl, a leggy blonde, a sports model, your best friend, that guy from the bowling alley (you didn't see that one coming, did'ya?) or just simply someone else to send you into a self-esteem spiral that can last for years. Then we end up in an ongoing cycle of losing romantically because every time a relationship or even a first date doesn't pan out, you blame yourself. The thought that runs through your head is: *"There must be something wrong with me because I wasn't good enough for them to love me."* What your thought should be is: *"I'm only responsible for my half of it, not his. It wasn't a match for me because it takes both halves for it work, so I'm better off for it ending now."* Do you know why that should be your thought? **BECAUSE YOU CAN'T LOOK FOR SOMEONE ELSE TO GIVE YOU YOUR VALUE!** You have to do that for yourself, you *CAN* do it for yourself and you certainly f***ing should.

Self-esteem, self-worth and confidence are things you have to constantly rebuild until you get to the place where those things can no longer be shaken from you. But these things are only are gained by a series of tiny victories that, once accumulated, start making you feel better about yourself. You can't wait for the world to drop these opportunities in your lap; you have to go and create those victories for yourself. "How do I do that?" Easy. Create small accomplishable victories that you can do on a daily basis and that you will under no circumstance deviate from. Personal hygiene is a great place to start. Every morning, wash your face: Victory! Brush your teeth: Victory! Floss: Victory! See? You've only been awake for ten minutes and are already winning. Boom. More victories for you, my friend! What we are talking about here are good choices, many of them in a row, which make you feel good about your self, thus blowing up your sagging self-esteem. Exercise, travel, find something that makes you feel great and do it—volunteer at a charity or take on a challenge that's achievable. But consistency is key. Tiny victories are what will nourish you back to the promise you once had. You have to do this or some version of this every day as a way of honoring who you are and how you operate. Your unwillingness to compromise will be your greatest asset because that is what tells you and the world that you care about yourself (which we all know is a huge turn-on). Tiny victories are actually the cornerstone of almost any successful person you know because when all else fails at least you flossed.

The key to Ultra-Successful Winner Dating is that you can't date what you are not. You will not attract great things by wishing for them, seeing a psychic or buying magic rocks. You only get Great by being Great, and Greatness takes work!

BUT GREG AND AMIIRA, I HAVE QUESTIONS!

BUT WHAT IF I'M NOT WORTHY?

Dear Greg and Amiira,

I was supposed to get married two Christmases ago to my boyfriend of three years, but about six months before the wedding he changed his mind. He said he didn't think he was in love with me. He's not with anyone else, but I can't get past the idea that there's something wrong with me. Why else would he break our engagement to be alone?

Kate
Bath, England

Dear Wedding Crashed,

It sucks to get dumped when you thought you had your whole life worked out, but what he actually did was the excellent service of not marrying you when he recognized that he wasn't in love with you. Despite what may have been in the past, things change and it sucks. However, it also means that you were released to move on to your next great thing, but you are holding up the bus by blaming yourself, sinking your self-esteem and being an all-around bummer. The only thing wrong with you is that you can't see your value, and that's going to take some work, possibly even counseling, but it's time to revisit the girl you were when you were at your best. Possibly right before you met the wedding smasher. Hang in there, Hot Stuff; your story ain't over yet.

BUT WHAT IF I CAN'T REBUILD MY SELF-ESTEEM?

Dear Greg and Amiira,

My last boyfriend cheated on me with some girl from his office. The boyfriend before that cheated on me with a mutual friend, and the boyfriend I had before that was just an asshole. I don't know why, but I stayed with all of these men for long after I had identified their problems. I don't know how to rebuild my self-esteem after so many blows to the ego.

Claire
Minneapolis, MN

Dear Loser Magnet,

Holy smokes! You do have the winning ticket to the loser lotto. Do you know the phrase "Water seeks its own level"? The same goes for losers. That doesn't mean that I'm calling you a loser, but what I am saying is that you are comfortable with them and you allow them to be the losers they are in your company. What that does mean is that there's something in your mechanics that tells you that you don't deserve better than this, and whatever that is needs a fixing. To rebuild your self-esteem you need to surround yourself with people that make you feel good and bring out the best in you, take care of your well-being without exception and line up some tiny victories. It's only when you get to the place where you think you're worthy of a good relationship that you'll find one. So kick the losers to the curb and get some help for whatever's ailing your self-worth.

BUT WHAT IF I DO LIKE MYSELF?

Dear G & A,

I'm 42 years old, I own my own company, I have a lot of great friends, a great relationship with my family, and I've lost over a hundred pounds in *the past year, so I'm in fantastic shape for the first time in my life. In other words, I'm not f***ed up. But I'm starting to feel like I'm going to spend my life alone. I go to clubs, bars, cocktail parties, dog parks, you name it, but no one seems to notice me and I can't get asked out. What do I do? I'm really lost in this part of my life.*

Anika

Ft. Lauderdale, FL

Dear Weighed Down,

Firstly, congratulations on doing so many things right in your life and taking control of your health and weight. Bravo to you. Here's what I think is happening: you're used to being overweight and probably have been overweight your whole life. So even though you like yourself and have shed the extra pounds, you still feel like the fat girl and probably carry yourself as such. That means you're projecting old ideas about yourself onto the new you and taking those out into the world, and people respond thusly. People aren't noticing you because you don't feel noteworthy still. So let's stop that business right now, because you didn't do all of that work to lose. If it means standing in front of the mirror every day or leaving yourself a voice message that says, "I am now a new person. Have you seen my butt?" then do it because, like every person reading this, you're great and you deserve to be in a great relationship, but it will only happen not only if you like yourself and feel worthy of it but project that out into the world as well.

BUT WHAT IF THERE'S NOTHING TO LIKE?

Dear Greggers and Amiiricle,

What's wrong with me? Why can't I catch a break? I always get "downsized" at jobs, dumped after the first date, or completely overlooked because my best friend is prettier than me. I'm the person that has to be thankful for bad luck; otherwise, I'd have no luck at all. Now there's this guy who I really like and he only knows me as the girl who dropped her new phone in the toilet at work. Why would he even like me, much less want to go out with me? For once I just wish something good would happen to the girl standing next to the pretty girl.

Florence

Quebec, Canada

Hey Flo,

Hard on yourself much? Look, being clumsy is fine, in fact it can be cute, but being clumsy or having bad luck is not your problem. You're treading water in a personal crisis because you don't even kind of like yourself or think you deserve good things. If you're running for the title in the Miss Victim Of Her Own Life you definitely have a good shot, but I'd suggest you step down from that pageant and try to get involved in the Miss I Like Myself competition. And by the way, who cares if your best friend is prettier than you, and why is it that you like her better than you like yourself? If you want anyone including the guy at work to like you, you have to start liking yourself first. As for the catching a break part, you have to make your own breaks and optimize those before the universe will start dropping them at your feet. So next time you drop your mobile phone down the toilet, just turn to the guy you like at work and playfully say, "Which do you think is hotter: that I dropped my phone in the toilet or that I went in after it?" Or, "I'd offer you my phone so you can call my voicemail to ask me out, but it's on vacation in the ladies room." Be confident, have a sense of humor about life's little trials and see if you can't give yourself a break!

FROM THE OTHER SIDE OF THE FENCE

BUT WHAT IF IT'S NOT ME, IT'S THEM?

Dear Greg and Amiira,

Women never like me, so dating sucks. I'm the assistant manager of a small women's boutique, so I'm around women all the time, and I overhear their conversations about men. You should hear the load of crap they say. They talk about not caring if guys have money and just wanting to be taken out on a real date. And then in the next sentence they talk about their expensive dates with the guys with money going to a fancy restaurant in town. They're all phonies. Where's the girl who is going to be super excited to go out for McRibs with me in my Honda when she could be out with some guy with money and a cool car? Seriously f*** it.

Brad

Fargo, ND

Dear Bad Braditude,

I hear you and I get what you are saying and I think you are right. You don't have enough money, so give up and stop dating altogether, then you'll have more time to pick out the small apartment where you are destined to die alone. (Make sure it has no windows or a view of the alley where the dumpsters are.) Or you can A) not worry about girls who are only interested in guys with money, B) figure out ways to be creative with the money you have and C) figure what kind of life you want to have. But before you do all that I'd say you should take a good long look at how you feel about women, because from your letter it seems like you hate all of them *as well as yourself.* With all due respect I don't know anyone that would sign up with some one-on-one time with that attitude and lack of self-esteem. You're surrounded by women all day—that's a giant opportunity that not all guys have, and if you took advantage of it and learned how to be charming and funny instead of pissed off at all the women you're surrounded by, you'd probably be in high demand for dates instead of being rejected by them. *And, by the way, there are far more attractive things than money, like confidence, for instance. You should try to get some of that. It'll get you further in life than a wad of cash.*

THE CHICK THAT ROCKED IT

I'm not going to pretend that I've never been the kind of guy that doesn't take advantage of a good opportunity with girls. I don't know if it's a "Daddy" thing or what, but some girls let you walk all over them or treat them like shit. When we were still in college the guys would all sit around and compare notes about it. So after college I expected that it would probably be different once I was in the business world working with professionals instead of Sorority girls. But even the most successful women are so starved for male attention that they'll let you go all the way without even promising them a phone call. It's wild. So I was riding the wave of no strings attached for many years until I met Susan. Susan wasn't having any of my bullshit and wasn't even kind of amused by it. For the longest time I couldn't figure out what it was that made her different, but I was so fascinated by her. She was smart, sexy and confident, which is great, but I had been with women like that before. She was pretty-ish but had a good size nose that she should have been self-conscious about but wasn't. I couldn't stop thinking about her, and she couldn't care less about me. I tell you I have never worked so hard for a first, second or third date as I did to get Susan to go out with me. The more time I spent with her the more I was intrigued by her, but it wasn't until years later when we were living together that I finally figured out why she was different from every girl I had ever dated before. She liked herself and didn't need my approval in the slightest bit. So I married her before she could realize that I lacked those qualities myself, and I hope that I somehow get to learn them from her before she figures me out. Why women settle for scraps I'll never understand, but as long as they do, guys are happy to reap the benefits from it.

Tim

Denver, CO

IT WORKED FOR ME!

I met you guys at a singles mixer for "It's Called A Breakup Because It's Broken" in Seattle. During a Q&A session I told you about my last relationship with a verbally abusive man and the subsequent breakup of it, and you were both very supportive of my decision to leave (a decision I was regretting at the time). When you spoke to me, one of you said that I didn't think I deserved anything better than being in an abusive relationship, and I told you that you were wrong. You continued to challenge me on that idea, and it really hurt my feelings because I like to think of myself as a pretty together person who likes herself. But when I got home that night I looked at the pictures in frames around my house, seeing images of myself as a little girl with my parents and at various stages of my life, and I burst into tears. I cried for a long time and it was a therapeutic crying jag, but during it or maybe what caused it was the realization that you were right. If I really felt like I deserved better, I wouldn't have stood for the abuse as long as I did, and it wouldn't have been hard to leave. So it's a few years later now and I've been doing a lot of work on myself and seeing a therapist to try to figure out why I constantly compromise myself for others that wouldn't do the same for me. I feel like a different person, a clearer person and a more confident and valuable person. Today I'm happy to write to you to tell you that I've met a wonderful man who loves and reveres me as much as I do myself, and we're getting married this fall. (Please see the enclosed invitation.) I hope you can attend because you really did change my life, but no need to bring a gift; you've already given me one.

Mavis

Kirkland, WA

FIRST PERSON SINGLE, BY AMIIRA

I settled for pieces of the pie for a long time in my romantic history. If there was a guy with only few of the qualities I was looking for but loads of the ones I wasn't then I was on board! Or better yet, if there was a guy who couldn't commit but could muster up just enough effort to string me along then sign me up! That's my man! But don't tell him he's my man because it might scare him off. Anything that felt bad and made me insecure was worth the effort, because if I could just get the person who doesn't love me to love me then I would know for sure that I am good enough. Good enough for what? Seriously. What is it that I'm looking for and why do I think that this asshole that makes me feel less than or inadequate is not only better than me but has the answers? Why does someone else hold the key to my self-esteem? That's the revelation I finally had after yet another disappointing quasi relationship with someone who had such bad qualities that it was almost comical. It takes one of those to give you the proverbial smack upside the head so that you can give your brain a good shake and get all the self-loathing out. You have to continually hit the reset button on your life to make you consciously start making better choices because no one else can do it for you. Look, it's hard to be in a relationship where there's an imbalance of feelings. I know it because I've been on both sides of that imbalance, and neither of them is really that comfortable. At least when you're the one least invested you don't feel the panic and inadequacy of when you're on the losing end of the "Please Love Me Enough" equation. But being uncomfortable in your relationship is symptomatic not only of the fact that you're in the wrong relationship but that you aren't in a good space with yourself. Continuing to be in bad relationships where you feel not good enough, unloved, and insecure or anything other than consistently great is like having a gambling addiction. Every day thinking the next will be the turning point where things will stabilize and be great is the same thing as thinking that the next hand of cards is going to make you the big winner when in fact you're just slowly giving yourself away. It's denial in a truly profound sense because you participate in it daily and you know it even if it's only on a gut level that shows itself in the discomfort you feel being riddled with self-doubt.

It's hard to say why it took me so long to like myself enough to gracefully refrain from engaging in self-doubting relationships, but once I had figured it out it was an undeniable truth that I could not turn back from. No one knows better than I do about me, and because of that I don't need anyone to validate me. I am free. I am powerful. I am worthy. I am loveable. And people around me know that *I know* that about myself. It only took me ten years to get there, but because I got there I found the best relationship for me, and now I get the rest of my life to feel good.

THOUGHTS FROM MAN CITY

What attracts a man to a woman? Cleavage! The End.

Okay, that's not really what I want to say. It's really an almost impossible question to answer. Probably because the answer lies in what each individual man is looking for. There are things we know for sure: Sex appeal is very high if not at the top of the list. Men are visual creatures. (See the Internet for details.) Confidence is also high on our list because it can almost completely make up for any shortcomings a person has in the looks department. Then there are things like personal style, work ethic (Yes, contrary to popular belief some men like a woman they have to compete with.), religious beliefs and favorite bands. But my note to you ladies is: **WHO GIVES A SHIT?** Finding out what we like won't help you unless you like it too. If you want to be in a great relationship then I suggest having a great relationship with yourself. We are only going to like you if you like you, and if you don't, we can tell. And some of us will prey on those weaknesses for our own pleasure. Do I have to explain or do you get it? When you compromise *your* values or *your* needs for *our* pleasure or attention, we will always sense it and eventually leave. It works both ways. Any time I ever gave up who I was to procure sex or attention it always ended badly. (See: *It's Called a Breakup Because It's Broken* for further details.) The only reason people compromise themselves is because they don't feel strongly enough about themselves and are looking for another person to fix it for them, either sexually or emotionally. That's why it is imperative that you get to a place where you like yourself, even if just for the added bonus of weeding out the creeps.

DATING FORTUNE COOKIE

Sexy beats cute, smart takes sexy, funny wins the pot ... and confidence body slams them all.

WORST DATE EVER

I never understood what I was doing wrong on dates until I went on a date with myself. Let me explain. About a year ago I met this guy on a chairlift skiing in Lake Tahoe. It was a long ride and on it I learned that he lived in San Francisco like I did. He asked me out, or rather hinted that he would like to ask me out, but he said he was too shy. I thought it was a kind of a cute way of asking/not asking me out. I know how you guys feel about that stuff, but he was really cute, so I helped him ask me out and we went on a date.

It was the worst date I'd ever been on. We had dinner at this really nice restaurant in the Embarcadero in San Francisco. It was all going okay, but he was very down and hesitant about things, and everything he said about himself was negative, like: "I don't know, I'm not really that smart"; "I used to be fit but now I'm in terrible shape"; "My life's not really that interesting"; or, "You're probably used to dating better-looking guys." Here he was, this handsome skier with a great job in real estate, and all he could do was tell me what a loser he was while putting away drink after drink and getting more and more depressed. It bugged me a lot, but then I finally realized that it bothered me because I had been guilty of doing the same thing for as long as I could remember. Constantly selling myself short, putting myself down for God knows what reason and falling apart on dates. You know what I found out? It's a big turnoff. No one wants to date a conceited ass, but who wants to date the person that thinks so little of herself? It was the very first time in my life that I realized that *I'm a beautiful skier with a great job, and despite what I've spent years telling date after date after date, I'm kind of a catch.* I didn't see him again, but I did see me and what a terrible date I had been for the first time, so the date wasn't a total loss.

IT'S JUST YOUR F***ING HAPPINESS

Your happiness is the most important thing in this life. If you are not happy, you are of no use to anyone else. Look, no one is happy all the time, but if you are in the pursuit of happiness, that's what will ultimately make you appealing to the kind of man that not only wants to stick around but is also fun to be with. The point is you have to figure out how to be happy no matter the cost, and we can tell you right here and now that happiness won't come from another person. It will come from the tiny victories and the big goals. Ultimately, if you find happiness you may find that you don't need a man in your life, and if you do find a great man, he is simply an addition to a life well lived.

THE ORIGINAL WORLD FAMOUS WINNER DATER'S WORKBOOK

It's time to get serious about reclaiming your self-esteem. Whatever your personal zenith was, whatever the time in your life where you were totally ruling, winning and firing on all cylinders—*that's where the answers are to reclaiming your self-worth.* That's where your self-esteem was the highest, when you were projecting that into the universe and having the most personal success. You have to go back to the point in your life where you felt the very best about yourself and figure out how you got there, what was going on for you then that isn't now, and how to get yourself back into that space. To find a great relationship it's imperative that you of all people believe all the best things about yourself again and figure out why those beliefs went away in the first place. Seriously, if you don't feel them then why would anyone else be able to feel that about you?

Bust out your laptop, a notebook, cocktail napkin or whatever you can find. It's personal inventory time. Fill in the blanks in the most specific terms you can. Let's see if we can't go and find the super you!

When was the best period in your life?

What was going on that made it great?

What was different about you then?

How did you feel about yourself then?

When did things change and what changed?

How do you feel about yourself now?

What can you actively do to get back into that space?

Let's build on the good stuff you already have going for you.

Why are you special?

What makes you different from everybody else?

Why are you a person of value that others should get involved with?

What are your best qualities?

What are your lovable flaws?

What are the tiny victories you're going to line up for yourself?

PRINCIPLE #2
GET A LIFE, HAVE A LIFE

AND DON'T GIVE IT UP FOR EVERY TOM, DICK AND AGNES THAT COMES ALONG

Dating someone new is always exciting. The rush of feelings you get accompanied by the desire to spend every minute together basking in the yummy gooey feelings of *first like* are awesome. It's like you've entered this utopian little existence where the two of you are in this bubble totally connected by these bursting emotions. You text constantly, see each other daily, run home from work to get to him five minutes earlier, blow off your friends, go into work late, leave early, skip your yoga class, and everything is great … until it all bites you in the ass. When you give up your life to devote all of your time and energy to a new romance you suffocate the other person. The feelings go from being "Wow, she's amazing" to "I can't get enough of her" to "She's a little needy and wants to spend every second with me" to "I can't get rid of her" to "How can I avoid her?"

You can feel the shift when someone is willing to give you all of their attention, and though at first it's flattering, shortly thereafter it becomes burdensome. It's those shifts that cause you to back off, or to have someone back off from you. We've all done it or felt it. People don't want you to give up your life for them even if they think they do at the beginning. Those that do want you to give yourself up for them are the ones that later will stalk you.

Many dating books, experts, websites and crystal balls suggest that you appear busy, ignore phone calls, pretend you have plans, and generally play a game called "*I don't have time for you; please fall in love with me.*" And while this may appear like sound or at least strategically sound advice, it is ultimately encouraging you to start off your relationship by being dishonest and has the faint smell of something … What is it? Oh, right, manipulation. That's how all of the great love stories start, right? Wrong. So why does it seem like it's the game of "*I don't have time for you; please fall in love with me*" would work? Well, it has a certain logic to it, being that you are hard to get and thusly more desirable, and because everybody wants what they can't have it makes sense that if you're unavailable then they'll want you more. But pretending you have a life is just pure game playing and misery. Well, then what is your magnificent suggestion, guys? Ready? Wait for it … GET A LIFE SO YOU WON'T HAVE TO PRETEND YOU HAVE ONE. Actually BE busy. Have unbreakable plans with your friends because they are as important as your love life. Be on time for work because it matters to you. Don't blow off your responsibilities, family, dreams, values or well-being for the next Jett, Kingston or Maddox that comes along.

People like a little mystery. People like to get to know you over a period of time, and they like to think about you and wonder what you might be doing. Wonder why you might have to leave early, why you like your job, why your friends are so important or why you're so close to your family and think, "*Wow, she's got other priorities than me and a very cool life.*" Having a life that's important to you and not dumping your friends, job, plans, interests and current schedule for someone new will serve BOTH of you well.

YOU MUST HAVE A LIFE! A full one that does not stop every time a potential boyfriend or girlfriend comes into the fray. And if you don't have one you need to ask yourself why that is and what the f*** you're waiting for? Seriously. There are people that live lives that people admire and there are people that watch people live those lives. Why are you being a watcher instead of a doer? It's actually quite simple to get a life. For instance let's say it's Thursday, and you don't have plans for Friday, but you think the person you have your sights on might call to ask you out. The old you would have just waited to see if they called then be disappointed if they didn't and have missed the boat on whatever opportunities you might have had besides a date. But the new you, being the doer that you are, will not sit by the phone but instead will make any variety of plans that will enrich your life or create an interesting experience to retell over coffee, like hooking up with old friends, trying a new restaurant, going to see a great new band at that club you've never been to, or attending an art opening. By getting out in the world and doing things instead of waiting for someone to take you into their world, you become a person that is living a fuller life. Are you not more interesting when you have experiences to share? Are you not more appealing if you have events to talk about it? Are you not more fascinating if you have a valuable life instead of a disposable one?

PEOPLE ARE ATTRACTED TO WINNERS AND MOVEMENT. We love and are inspired by people who move gracefully through this world with a sense of purpose. People who don't ask permission to live their lives but actually just do it regardless of what others think. When you have a full life, not only will you attract the things you want but you'll also still get to have the things you have.

BUT GREG AND AMIIRA, I HAVE QUESTIONS!

BUT WHAT IF HIS SCHEDULE IS HARD TO WORK AROUND?

Dear Greg and Amiira,

I've been going out with a guy for a couple of weeks who works a lot. He can't plan ahead that often for dates, so I've been really cool about keeping my schedule open in case he can see me. My friends are getting all pissed off at me because I either won't commit to plans with them or bail to see the new guy. What's the trick to this sticky situation?

Clara

Notting Hill, England

Dear Calendar Girl,

Let me put it this way. We fly Virgin Airlines because we like them and they are dependable. However, they don't wait for us to call to decide when they are going fly. They have a schedule to keep, so we fly only when it's right for both of us, not just them. Sometimes we have to change our plans so we can catch a certain flight because we don't want to fly with anyone else. We also know that if we decide not to fly they are going to fly anyway and that doesn't mean they don't like us. It means they've got a job to do, and that's why we fly them in the first place. Plus they are just a really sexy airline. Do you see where we're going with this? You are the airline. You should keep your flights—that means plans with your friends and your own schedule. He can come fly with you when he can, but you aren't holding up the plane or your life for him. Because flying with you is better than flying any other airline, and the right guy will figure that out.

BUT WHAT IF I'M HAPPY TO GIVE UP MY LIFE?

Dear Greg and Amiira,

When I like someone, I like them A LOT! I can't help the way I feel and I'm not going to deny myself all those great feelings when you like someone new and are completely inseparable. I'm happy to give up my life because what I get in return is worth the price. I'm guilty of smothering guys but I've been smothered too, and it's not the worst way to figure out that you're not in the right thing. That's how I roll, and it just makes sense to me that when I find the right guy we'll be all over each other and know we're in the right relationship when neither of us gets tired or smothered. That sounds like paradise to me. Every relationship is a gamble, and I'm a girl with a stack of chips and a taste for gambling. So put that in your pipe and smoke it.

Brooke

Los Angeles, CA

Dear Smoking Aces,

Right on. Can't wait until your book comes out. Sounds like you and the guys you attract have a lot going for you.

P.S. The next time you smother someone do it with a pillow, that way they'll never go away.

WHAT IF NOT CANCELING MY PLANS DOESN'T WORK?

Dear Greg and Amiira,

I went on this fabulous first date with a sports writer. This was on a Monday. I felt we really connected. We both like Gastropubs, the outdoors, and especially camping. He actually said something like, "We should go camping sometime." Which I thought was both promising and sweet. So I said, "… let me check my schedule." We laughed about it. Two nights later he took me to a Pirates game, and the night after that we went dancing. Both times he brought up the camping thing, even saying maybe we could go that weekend. I told him I had a cousin who was having her baby shower but maybe the weekend after that. He said that he was going to be on the road with the Pirates and that this was the only chance he'd have for awhile. I told him I wasn't going to break my plans but would block out some time when he got back. He agreed but I never heard from him again. Did I blow it? I really liked him.

Emily
Pittsburg, PA

Dear Camp Emily,

You did blow it. Not only should you have told your cousin to shove it, you should have also quit your job, bought a tent and camped out in front of his place. No, you didn't blow it! You did exactly what you should have done, which is stick to your plans. You had already seen him three times that week. The fact that you never heard back makes us think that the sports writer just wanted to get you naked in a tent. Otherwise, he would have gladly waited for the pleasure of your awesome company. Besides, how upset would you be had you disappointed your cousin, gone camping and then he never called again? Just keep doing what your doing, kiddo, because you're batting a thousand.

WHAT IF HE HAS NO LIFE?

Dear Greg and Amiira,

Okay, here's a tough one. I've been seeing this very cool guy for a little over a month. He did everything right, in fact he is just that into me. Ha! He calls, he shows up when he says he's going to, he's affectionate, he's interested in my work (I'm a litigator), and he likes my friends and family.

So what's the problem? I feel so bad even writing this, but he's too available. I was so afraid he was going to be like so many guys I had dated before that weren't interested in my life, but this is just the opposite. He's almost too interested in my life; not only that, but aside from his job (he's a systems analyst) he doesn't seem to have a life of his own. How do you tell someone to get a life? I don't want him to ruin this. How do I fix it?

Cameron
Cardiff, Wales

Dear He's Just Too Into You,

You just have to tell him the truth today because this is a relationship killer. Here's how you do it: You tell him all the good things you just told me about him and that this relationship has real potential, but in order for it to go the distance, he shouldn't feel the need to devote so much time to you. Tell him that you'd love to do more things with his friends and family and that you also require a little alone time to recharge your battery. One of two things will happen: He will be excited at the possibility of bringing your two worlds together, or you'll find out for sure that he has no other life. If the latter is true, then you will have to tell him that your requirements for a great relationship include both people having a full life and that he's got to find other things in his life besides his job and you to bring him happiness. Hopefully he will understand. You may be doing him a giant favor, but you have to be clear that this relationship will not work unless he does that. Sorry, hot stuff, but it just won't.

FROM THE OTHER SIDE OF THE FENCE

WHERE CAN I FIND A LIFE?

Dear Greg and Amiira,

I heard you on the radio the other day talking about getting a life, but you didn't say exactly how one should do that. Here's my problem. I moved recently for work and within a week I met the girl who would become my girlfriend. We spent all kinds of time together, but now I can tell she's getting kind of sick of me. I don't want to be that guy who has no life. The problem is I don't know anyone here except my boring office mates, and most of my social life revolves around her. Help.

Burton
Roswell, GA

Dear This Boys Life,

Softball, guitar lessons, training for a 10K, charity work—just do something. Look, moving is a big adjustment, let alone adding a new relationship to the mix. So do some deep thinking. Get a piece of paper and write down all the things you have always wanted to try or do. Anything from starting a band to losing weight is an excuse to get you out the door and into the world. Plus, don't be afraid to spend some time alone. Trust us, as the married parents of two, we read your letter with a spot of envy. We love our life like no other, but there are days when we'd eat a bee's nest for a couple hours alone. Okay, that's not entirely true but you get our gist.

THE CHICK THAT BLEW IT

Sienna and I worked for the same Internet marketing company for about two years, but I only ever spent time around her at company functions, retreats, team building events, etc. … Then I got promoted and ended up being in charge of her division. I thought, "Cool, now I'll get to know her better." So I asked her out, and we went on a few dates that were great. I realized that I really like her a lot and I wanted to see her all the time. I'd call her from business meetings and ask her to sneak out to meet me during work hours, but she wouldn't. It was delicious torture. We'd meet up after work a couple times a week, but that was it. She and her sister have dinner together on Tuesdays, she has Pilates on Thursdays, does her laundry and housekeeping on Sunday, and had just signed up for a pottery class Saturday morning. She was pretty scheduled out, so that didn't leave that much time for me. Finally a girl with a life of her own, how sexy is that? I was really getting into her and loved having to juggle my own schedule to snake any openings she had. It made the time we did spend together really valuable. But then it's like she flipped a switch and just ditched everything to hang out with me all the time. She even blew off her Tuesday dinners with her sister and was just always there. All the things that made her so interesting and almost unattainable were just gone. I tried to hang in there, but when she stopped doing all those things she stopped being the girl I was so attracted to and became totally dependent on me to fill her time. It was too much pressure and I bailed.

Enzo
Berkley, CA

IT WORKED FOR ME!

I spent years being unfulfilled by my life, my job, my boyfriends and my friend-friends. I just couldn't get everything in sync to a place where it all felt good instead of just okay. So now I'm here. I love my job and get great satisfaction from doing it well. I've narrowed down my friends to just the ones where the friendship is effortless, secure and supportive. I have a dog that keeps me busy and well loved and have my little rituals that I do, whether they're bubble baths, crossword puzzles, Sunday matinees with the girls, or riding my bike to work once a week that make me feel pretty happy on a daily basis. Things felt better than good because I like my life. So when Mitchell and I started dating I was really reluctant to give any of it up because I had worked so hard to find the perfect balance in my life. It was the first time ever that I wasn't trying to escape from my life into a relationship. But Mitchell not only didn't want me to give up my life, he liked that about me and even had his own that he didn't want to give up. What a concept! Because we both had lives that we liked, we didn't just rush into spending all our time together and have really built our relationship slowly. The time we spend together is time we're dying to spend together because we have so much to tell each other and have had time (even if it's just been a day) to miss each other. It's the best-feeling relationship I've ever had and it's because my boyfriend is part of my life, not my life.

Gerilyn
Edmonton, Canada

FIRST PERSON SINGLE, BY AMIIRA

I like being alone; in fact, I love it, so when I was single it was a great luxury for me to get to design my life around the basic parameters of work, friendships and spare time. Though I've never been one to go to the movies or dinner at a restaurant on my own, I was always up for a solo adventure in the city and found that I often preferred being alone to having plans. How antisocial, right? Maybe or maybe not … The thing about having things that are important to you that don't depend on anyone else's availability or interest is that you can fuel your life and happiness without others. That in my estimation is a very powerful thing to be able to do. I'm very in touch with what makes me feel good, less than good, powerful and pathetic. Filling my life with things, people, events, pastimes and hobbies of value made my life and my time valuable. It also made it something worth building on instead of scrapping every time I had a good date. Not only that, I didn't need a man in my life to make my life great and found quite a few of them actually just complicated and detracted from it, which is definitely not a bonus to what I already had going on. My advice to anyone who is living a life that they don't love is to change it! If you don't like your job, find another one that you will like. If you don't like your wardrobe, get creative and make it better (*Project Runway*, anyone??). If you don't like your friends, the color of your apartment, the stuff you put in your fridge, the way you go to work, whatever the hell it is—it's up to you to improve it and mold it into something that you genuinely like. It's only when you get a good life, have a good life and maintain a good life that you'll find a man that is worth spending time away from it.

THOUGHTS FROM MAN CITY

I like the chase. I always have; the more challenging the course the more rewarding the catch. I don't care if it's an antiquated thought. And I believe it to be true for most men. When I've told women this they always respond with, "Well, I don't want to come off like a bitch that doesn't have time for the guy I like." You don't have to be a bitch about it. There is a nice way of letting someone know your life matters to you. If I look back the great loves of my life, they were always women who were self-possessed, confident and goal oriented. They were women who challenged me. I remember I dated a painter who, when she was working on a painting, wouldn't see me until it was done. Sometimes that would take weeks. Weeks! If I were lucky she'd let me visit her at bartending gig where she would make out with me for ten minutes in the utility closet before sending me home. That's it. But I was fascinated with her. So why didn't it work out with any of the other women? Because usually I'd end up giving my life away or being okay with seeing someone for only ten minutes a week in a utility closet. For a relationship to really work it has to be the coming together of two great, very valued lives that over a period of time merge while staying true to who they are. It's great when we fall in love with you, but it's even better when we fall in love with your life as well.

DATING FORTUNE COOKIE

You are the architect of your own life, so build one that you love living in … and put in a pool and a walk-in closet while you're at it.

WORST DATE EVER

Every year my girlfriends and I go to Las Vegas for our Ladies Weekend. I know it sounds a little corny, but I love blackjack and a good martini. I'm not a big partier; I'm a lab tech at a veterinary hospital and I'm studying to be a vet. So needless to say I really look forward to our girls getaway, and last year was no exception as my father had passed away and I really needed to do something fun. Well, about a week and a half before our big event I met Kurt when he brought his dog Cheech in for some X-rays. He was very handsome and talked to me like no man had spoken to me in some time. Since my divorce I really have spent the last few years working on myself and not really dating. Anyway, I was pretty taken with him. He took my number and we talked on the phone every night. I even came into work late a few times because I'd only gotten off the phone hours before. He was all I could think about. He finally asked me out and I'll bet you can guess for when. The same weekend as our Vegas trip! I told him I was so conflicted. He even said we could do it when I got back. I called my girlfriends and they all said the same thing. "He'll be here when you get back." That's why I'll never understand why I did what I did next ... I called him and told him I'd gladly break my plans to see him. Now that you know the deal you can only imagine how stupid I felt when he told me at dinner that he wanted to be clear that this was just a friend thing. A F***ING FRIEND THING! My girlfriend just now texts me that she's sitting next to Britney at the Palms and you want to be friends? How much worse does it get? Trust me, I learned my lesson.

IT'S JUST A F***ING ART MUSEUM

It's all out there waiting for you, kid. Museums, gyms, friendships, charities, travel, etc. ... all you have to do is put one foot in front of the other ... These are the things that make you attractive, these are things that give you stories to tell on dates, and this is life that awaits you. It is the life you must have in order to be in a successful relationship, so start taking some risks. You are not going to love everything you try, but do it anyway, because you never know who else signed up for that Formula One racing class.

THE ORIGINAL WORLD FAMOUS WINNER DATER'S WORKBOOK

It's time for you to get a life and if you already have one, it's time to make it an even fuller and more kick ass one. We are put here on this planet to explore and enjoy it, so let's get you out into it and doing things so that next time you get asked out you'll have to check your schedule *for real.*

Make a list of things that you want to do and start scheduling them regularly so that you are getting the most our of your life while this time is still yours alone to use. We'll give you a few ideas to start, but it's up to you to think of more then go do them regularly.

List 5 things you'd like to do weekly

    1. Take a yoga class

    2. Do the Sunday crossword puzzle

    3. Take the dog on a walk

    4.

    5.

List 5 things you'd like to do every other week

    1. See a movie

    2. Wander around Target for an hour

    3. Have dinner with a friend

    4.

    5.

List 5 things you'd like to do monthly

    1. Get your car washed

    2. Try a new restaurant

    3. Take a tennis lesson

    4.

    5.

PRINCIPLE #3
PRETTY IS AS PRETTY DOES

What's the Message You're Sending to the World?

So as it turns out, this world here that we've been living in happens to be a visual medium. How totally random is that? Not random at all actually. The reason we have eyes is to see the world around us and the people in front of us. To give our brains images and information so that it has things to process so that we can form opinions and ideas about what and who we see. But what does that mean to a dating book? Glad you asked, because we've been meaning to talk to you about this, and it's a bit awkward but … it's time to get real about what you're putting out into the world. We all have blind spots and don't necessarily see ourselves the way others see us, and we don't always care about the things that others care about. But the undeniable truth is that how you present—that means what you look like, how you're groomed, what you wear, how you smell, how you act, and how you carry yourself—speaks volumes to those that we come in contact with. We know, we know … people shouldn't be judged by the way they look but rather by what's on the inside. You're totally right and also totally in denial about how the world works.

Like it or not, men are visually stimulated creatures. Do you really think that when a guy sees two women—one of them styled out and groomed and feeling great, the other not particularly caring about what she looks like—that he thinks that the unstyled one must have a great personality? NO! He thinks the styled out girl might be interesting and the other one doesn't really care, so why should he? It's not about being pretty; it's about telling the world that you care about yourself. There's a million different ways to style out and make the effort; not everybody has to look like Kate Upton. And not looking like Kate Upton isn't a good excuse to not care how you look. Everyday you have to Outdress the Enemy! The Enemy is anyone (including yourself) who is getting in the way of your happiness. Every day you have to go out into the world dressed in the armor that prepares you for battle. You never know when you're going to meet the person who will change your life, or run into an ex. Either way, you want to look like the best version of you so that you are walking through the world with your head held high, a spring in your step and confidence oozing from every cell of your being. We're not saying that life is meant to be a battle, but some days feel like it. Why not up your game so that it's less of one? Check out *www.outdresstheenemy.com* for more on that.

Here are a few things to keep in mind ...

FEELING PRETTY IS PRETTY

If you know that plucking your eyebrows and shaving your legs make you feel prettier, then do it! If shaving your legs opens up your wardrobe to wearing skirts more often, then do it! Maybe you don't wear makeup because it adds time to your morning routine, but when you do wear mascara and lip gloss you look prettier, more noticeable and carry yourself with a little more sparkle. Men notice sparkle! So take the extra five minutes and then you won't have to wait until you're stuck in an elevator during a citywide blackout for someone to take an interest in getting to know you.

DON'T FORGET YOU'RE A WOMAN

Men like you to look nice and smell good; otherwise, they don't get to be distracted from their stupid problems when you walk by. They like to see your legs, catch a glimpse of your cleavage, watch you brush your hair away from your eyes, and most of all *they like to know that you know that you're a sexual being.* Any hint of sexuality or sensuality is golden with men.

BUT NOT A PROSTITUTE

Men want to see your body BUT not too much of your body! Do you know what we're talking about? There's a difference between making an effort to style out with your appearance and dressing *too sexy*. Some outfits tell a guy "Hey, it's cool to call me at 4:00 a.m.," and others say, "You are going to have to work for it if you want to be a part of this spectacular-ness!" Yes, spectacular-ness is a new word.

DATING ALERT

Dressing too sexy is a very real problem for a lot of women trying to attract someone that wants to *date* them. It's a fine line between dressing provocatively and dressing too sexy. When you fall on the side of too sexy you attract guys that just want to get laid and think you're the gal for the job. How can you tell if you're being too sexy? Well, are you revealing *all* of your physical assets? Is there enough skin to shock your father? That may be too sexy. Unless you're on stage performing at the Grammys, a burlesque show or in a Vegas chorus line you need not give away the North *and* South Poles. We suggest you choose a sexy part to feature instead of showcasing them all. Do you know how much sexier you are if a guy has to imagine what might be under those clothes? If he can see it, he doesn't have to imagine it, which means he's not getting the opportunity to really think about you.

IT'S NOT JUST ABOUT YOUR BODY

Take a good look at your life. What does the state of your car say about you? Is it clean and orderly, or can you write your name in the dirt and make a killing with the recycling in the backseat? What does your home look like? Is it cluttered, messy and reeking of old take-out or is it clean, organized and an inviting space to be in? What does the top of your desk at work look like? The reason we ask you to look at these things and take an honest inventory about what state they're in is because all of those things—your appearance, your home, your car, your dress, your office—tell someone not only what your life looks like but who you think you are and whether or not you value and like yourself. That's what people are going to base their opinions of you on whether what you're projecting is an accurate representation or not. If the guy of your dreams walked into your apartment, would he be impressed to see the piles of stuff on every surface and seventy-five framed pictures of your ex-boyfriend? Would super-handsome bachelor #1 be turned on by your teddy bear collection and cotton candy-pink sheets? Would your dreamboat delight in the idea of canoodling on a sofa covered in cat hair? How would it make you feel if you had a great date, then he walked in to your home, took a look around and decided that he didn't like your life? Everyone's sofa tells a story. What's your sofa saying? So with that said, what is it that you could be doing better? What is it that you need to change or work on?

This is a really hard chapter to write because no one wants to tell another human being that they're not good enough as-is. And that's not the message of this chapter, because we do think you're good enough as-is, but if you're reading this book it's because you're having trouble finding the right guy that echoes that same sentiment. It's hard enough to find each other in this world, so step up your game so that the message you project is "I might be the one" instead of "don't notice me" or even the popular trend of "I'm easy to get in the sack." We know you are smart, funny, cool, loyal, dorky, successful, compassionate, great in bed and all the other things that are important to be and, yes, that should be enough to find the right guy. And we agree that in a perfect world we all have laser beam vision or retinal scans where we can see into each other's hearts, souls and minds and find each other that way, but until that technology is perfected you're going to have to make the effort the old-fashioned way. What if the right guy for you can't find you among the sea of other women that don't try to stand out to him? Then what happens?

The image you project is important. Think about it … They don't make James Bond movies about a guy in flip-flops.

BUT GREG AND AMIIRA, I HAVE QUESTIONS!

WHAT IF THE THING I'M PUTTING OUT THERE ATTRACTS THE WRONG GUYS?

Dear Greg and Amiira,

So after my last breakup I really took stock and realized that, while I hadn't picked the greatest guy around, I also had some areas that needed work. So I joined a gym, got a new apartment and started seeing a therapist. My old boyfriend used to complain that I wasn't sexy enough, and in retrospect I have to agree. I was overweight and dressed dowdy, but now that I'm slimmer, I've started to dress sexier. I even highlighted my hair blond. I definitely feel pretty great about my transformation, but now the problem I'm having is that when I go to clubs, bars and the like I always get the guys that want to only have sex with me. What's a girl to do?

Portia

Stockholm, Sweden

Dear Stocks and Blondes,

First, we hope you can see that we're holding up a huge banner that says Portia Kicks Ass! We applaud your very smart response to the dissolution of your last relationship. It's so great to hear someone acknowledge her part in a breakup. Yes, he was the wrong guy, but we love that you were interested in what you could be doing better. Now it's just a matter of refinement. Look, since we have no idea what you look or dress like, let us just say this. There is sexy (Eva Mendes, Gwen Stefani, Beyoncé, Sophia Lauren) and there's "what time is the porn shoot." We're all for personal freedom in dress, but try and understand what you are putting out into the world. If you just want to get laid then rock the house. But if that's not what you're going for, and we assume it's not, then ask a good friend, "Is this dress gynecologically short?" or, "How much of my nipple is too much?" Look in magazines and find looks you like and try and replicate them. At the very least it's your right to tell men, "Hey, if you want to see more you're going to have to work a lot harder than that. This is the trailer for a movie that opens in a month."

BUT WHAT IF I'M NOT PRETTY?

Dear Greg and Amiira,

I am no Angelina Jolie. You can dress me up, put me in hair and makeup, and I'll look fine, but as soon as the "costume" comes off you are stuck with plain old ugly me. So why should I pretend to be what I am not … pretty? At least this way, men know what they're getting so they are not disappointed later.

Danica
Perth, Australia

Dear Costume Party,

Whatever works for you, Danica, but what doesn't work for us is how you feel about yourself. Our guess is makeup or no makeup, you are not a lot of fun to be around. We all look different without our hair gel, good pants, makeup or whatever. I think it's generally understood that most people don't look as good wet from the shower as they do when they arrive at the party, but that's not what people respond to. People don't fall in love with or even want to ask out your eyeliner; they simply notice you because you wore it, but your winning (read: not surly) attitude is what makes them like you.

BUT WHAT IF I'M STYLISTICALLY IMPAIRED?

Dear Greg and Amiira,

I know I'm supposed to style out more, I get that, but I hate shopping and I have no sense of style. Seriously, even if I had all the money in the world I'd just buy jeans and sweats. Where I live polar fleece is as fashionable as anything else. I have a decent body but I'm not a girly girl, and I'm lost in a department store. It bums me out because I know what you are saying about looks and personal presentation mattering, but I am clueless in this area.

Kendra
Seattle, WA

Dear Styleless in Seattle,

Man, we wish we could help you and take you shopping but sadly, we don't live near you. But you know who does? The jillions of people employed by department stores, the Gap, Urban Outfitters and other such establishments whose sole purpose is to help you find something to wear. There are people in hair salons, gyms, yoga studios and makeup counters whose whole lives are dedicated to making you look and feel better. So ask for help from people who can help you. Maybe you have a real stylish friend who would just jump at the chance to rock the mall with you. And do some research, look through one of those glossy fashion magazines or music magazines and start tearing out things you respond to. Even if you are not a girly girl there is something called Tomboy Chic. See any non-Red Carpet photo of Kristen Stewart for reference.

BUT WHAT IF THE IMAGE I'M TRYING TO PROJECT IS ECLIPSED BY MY WHEELCHAIR?

Dear Amiira & Greg,

Here's a question for you. I am paralyzed from the waist down, so obviously I'm in a wheelchair. I'm a very positive person and a super fun hang but let's get real, I am definitely at a disadvantage in the looks department just by virtue of my situation. It's hard to get psyched to go out when you won't even be a consideration in the first place. What does a girl like me do?

Violet
Baltimore, MD

Dear Wheels of Steel,

We would give the same advice to you as we would give to anyone else. What is the most rocking version of you? How do you look best? What's the coolest chair you could have? Have you changed you hair lately? We can't begin to imagine what your life is like, but we're guessing you have to work harder in all areas of your life, and dating is for sure going to be one of them that will require the same hard work. In our travels we have met and seen some very foxy wheelchair-bound ladies, so we know it's possible to achieve. And here's another thing to think about—all that is the easy stuff; you've already done the hard work by being so positive.

FROM THE OTHER SIDE OF THE FENCE
WHAT IF THE GIRL OF MY DREAMS IS BEAUTIFUL BUT HER LIFE IS A MESS?

Dear Greg and Amiira,

So, dude, I've been seeing this girl for a couple of weeks now. She is really hot. I mean f***ing Maxim/FHM magazine hot. But there's something about her that bums me out. The first few times we went out I drove, but then last Friday she wanted to take me out, so we took her car. It was a dump on wheels. Seriously, I've never seen so much crap in a car; it's like she's homeless, and I don't mean that to be mean. I even asked her if she really had an apartment. Then I began to notice other stuff, stuff like her re-wearing the same skirt three days in a row even when it had a stain on it. Look, I'm no neat freak, but I actually pulled gum out of her hair the other day. The thing is she's really funny and I'm falling for her, but I'm afraid when I see her apartment I'm going to want to run. Advice, bro?

Travis

Gnome, Alaska

Dear Gum Picker,

Greg here. I'm going to field this one because I had a similar situation with a girl I dated right after college. Your instincts about her apartment are probably right on. Her car is telling not only what her apartment may look like but really the inside of her head. The two things I can tell you are do not overlook this hoping it will just go away, and you can't change another person; they will only change when they want to. Because you are a good guy, your instinct is probably to rush in there and save this beautiful disaster, but you can't. The best thing you can do, and I know this will be hard, is tell her you think her car is too messy. You can offer to help her clean it. But the best thing you can do if you are really connecting with her is to tell her it bums you out and you can't hang with it. That may be the wake-up call she needed.

THE GUY THAT BLEW IT
AND THE CHICK THAT ROCKED IT

Jules and I have been friends for five and a half years. She's my best girl friend, she's like a sister to me, and we hang out all the time. We go to clubs together, rock shows, movies, you name it we do it, and she's always my "Wing Man" helping me pick up chicks and telling them how great a guy I am. So about three weeks ago when we were out she met this guy that she liked, and the next thing you know she's completely changed the way she looks. This is a girl who has never worn a dress in the five plus years that I've known her, and now she's in dresses and high heels. She's wearing cute little Natalie Portman outfits, wearing makeup, wearing her hair down, and she's HOT! Like really hot. Like, not the same person hot. Now I like her differently and I'm jealous that she's dressing up for some other guy and not me. I've never even thought about Jules and I being together, but now it's all I can think about. She's already my best friend, so it's not like I only like her for her looks, but I just see her so differently now that it makes me feel differently about her. I think I'm in love with my best friend now, and she's hot for someone else.

Joey
Glendale, AZ

IT WORKED FOR ME

You can go ahead and say, "I told you so," because you were right. The way you look matters. There, I said it. I was one of those too-cool-to-care-how-I-looked girls that wanted to prove the world wrong by not trying to make myself look pretty to get the guy. So I slugged out that brilliant plan for a few years and suffered about a million disappointments when the guys I liked only liked me as a friend. So I decided to do a little experiment and change one thing about what I wear and one thing about how I look. So instead of wearing loose fitting jeans and a loose fitting t-shirt I started wearing a cute and better fitting (not super tight!) tank top. Instead of wearing no makeup I started wearing lipgloss. Almost immediately guys started responding differently. So then I started wearing better fitting jeans with my cuter tops and wearing mascara and a little eyeliner. Now guys that didn't give the time of day were giving me free coffee at the coffee shop and totally flirting with me. And I not only like how I look and how looking prettier makes me feel, but I also still feel like me. It's not like I had to radically change who I am and become some hoochie to get a guy's attention. I just feel like a cuter version of me that's still being me, and it only takes like a few minutes more to look AND FEEL good. I truly didn't think a tube of lipgloss and better fitting clothes would make any difference, but I was wrong because I feel different and people see me differently and, all in all, I'm happier now.

Mallory
Puerto Vallarta, Mexico

FIRST PERSON SINGLE, BY AMIIRA

I met Greg Behrendt three times before I really noticed or remembered him even though he always remembered me. The first time was at a party and I was decked out all cute, the second time I was at a music convention for work so I was kind of hipstered out, but the third time I met Greg was at a hair salon on a weekday morning at 10:00 a.m. Now, when going to a hair salon for cut and color on weekday morning at 10:00 a.m. one doesn't usually shower since you're about to get your hair washed anyway. One also doesn't usually worry about what one's wearing as you will be changing into a robe upon arrival or draped in a smock. So here I am, rolling into the hair salon on a day off from work, unshowered and kicking it casual because it's not like I'm going to be seeing anyone I know—it's a workday, right? Nope. I'm there for all of five minutes before I feel someone staring at me. I look up and see Greg Behrendt's smiling face and he says, "Hey, I know you." I don't recognize him (again), so he explains how I had come to a party at his house with a mutual friend and then how we had met again in Seattle at the Bumbershoot festival. So we exchange pleasantries and are chatting it up, and I'm thinking that he's pretty funny and easy to talk to. Well, since we were both getting highlights in our hair, we both spent hours at the salon. Sometimes sitting side by side under hair dryers while our colors processed, others separated by the distance between our respective hairdresser's workstations. Now take a moment to picture me (not that he was any better): I've got my hair separated into sections and wrapped in foil, a clear shower cap over the foils with cotton balls unrolled and placed along my front hairline, and I'm draped in a black nylon smock that comes down to my knees. So basically my feeling hot factor wasn't off the charts and I was carrying some pretty severe aesthetic obstacles. But because I don't ever leave the house unless I feel a little cute (because who wants to go into the world losing from the get-go?) I had taken the time to put on a little mascara and lip gloss, and under my smock my outfit had some personality. So between having a little cuteness in my holster, which gave me some confidence that I might not have had in that situation, combined with a healthy dose of conversation and "get to know you time" and *despite* having with my hair in foils, covered in a shower cap while sitting under a hair dryer wearing a black nylon smock, he asked me to come see him do stand-up later that night.

THOUGHTS FROM MAN CITY

I'm not a pretty man. I've got a long face, a weak jaw, big nose, a lazy eye and mousy blond hair that looks "okay" in one direction. My hips are wider than my shoulders, I have tiny ladylike hands and I'm pale. Oh, I also look bad in hats, helmets, do-rags, vertical stripes, cowboy boots and boatneck collars. And I wouldn't change places with anyone. I love me. I am my own personal challenge. My job while I'm on this earth is to take this body, mind and soul and to shape it into a useful human being. So I take excellent care of myself. I see my weaknesses as my strengths and I have spent a lifetime honing them. Because I wasn't the best-looking guy I tried to be the funniest. Because I didn't have the best body I tried to dress it better than everyone else. In essence I got it. I got the message early on. I, like most people, have had to work at it and because I did, people have noticed. We, as in we men, notice you. We notice what you look like, we notice what you wear, we notice when you're laughing, we notice when you care about yourself. We notice when you take the time to look good and we love it when you do. When you don't take the time, when you don't put the effort into how you look, then usually we don't notice you. It's as simple as that.

DATING FORTUNE COOKIE

You don't have to be pretty to be attractive.

ONE OF GREG'S
WORST DATES EVER

When I first moved to San Francisco after college, I met this beautiful girl who lived on my block. She was playwright and waitress. I asked if she wanted to go for a late cup of coffee one night. She agreed and asked if I'd stop by her place to pick her up. I arrived when she asked me to at nine o'clock, and she came to the door in a robe saying she'd just woken from a nap. She invited me in and said she wouldn't be a moment. Her apartment was a mess, and when I say that I don't mean mess in the traditional sense of busy young bohemian with a lot on her plate messy, I mean indoor junkyard "are those eyeballs in those jars?" messy. I mean, "what's that smell and does it have its own driver's license?" messy. And I kid you not, she walked down the hall in her robe and picked up the panties that were lying on the floor by a soiled plate and slid them on. This is before we've had a formal hello. Now, look, I didn't expect every person I dated to feel the same way about hygiene as me. I wasn't even a neat freak back then, but this was a lot to ask a person you don't know to be okay with. I got a peek into her world that I wasn't ready for. I judged her because of it, and I'll tell you why: most of the people I know who live like that are really sad and messed up, and I saw it as a warning sign. The fact that I think she forgot we were even supposed to go out made our first date our last. Wherever she is now, I hope at least she has some clean underwear.

IT'S JUST F***ING PULLING IT TOGETHER

Look, you really can't argue against looking better regardless of what your version of you looking good is. Yes, it takes a little effort, but so does practically everything else in life that's worth having. Besides, when you look good, you feel good and when you feel good, you attract good things. But more importantly, when *you* think you're worth the effort and you make the effort—so will others. Try it our way and see if you don't agree. There is a fantastic version of you in there, and we want to see it go on a date. Even at the end of the day (date or no date) you still honored yourself and pulled yourself together, so it wasn't a complete loss.

THE ORIGINAL WORLD FAMOUS WINNER DATER'S WORKBOOK

Have you ever had a friend tell you, "I'm doing everything I can but I'm just not finding anyone," but when you look at that person you know they're not doing everything they can. They might be overweight, not be a good listener, have stinky breath and bad manners. In essence you know what their problem is, and if you had the guts you'd tell them, but you don't want to hurt their feelings or upset them. We've all been there. Now we're asking you to turn that mirror on yourself and be honest about it … could you use a mint?

Do you put the time into your appearance that you should?

Is the image you project to the world one that says, "I'm worth getting to know"?

What could you be doing better to make yourself more interesting to the people you want to attract?

What is it that you need to change or work on?

Once you've truthfully answered these questions, you'll be able to see where you need improvement to better yourself and your chances for attracting the guy that's been out there looking for you. So get your act together, whiten your teeth, shave your legs, pluck your brows, put on some kick ass shoes and let him know you're here!

PRINCIPLE #4
DON'T ACCEPT LESS THAN AN ACTUAL DATE

Stop Selling Yourself Short!

There are dates … and then there are things that appear to be dates, feel like dates or even have elements of a date but **ARE NOT** dates. We know you know what we're talking about because that's what you and your friends have been settling for, then trying (unsuccessfully) to parlay these non-dates into a relationship. So unless you're having a yard sale where you're selling yourself short, as of now you will not be going on NOT-dates, quasi dates, half-assed dates or semi-sort of couldabeen dates ever again (*This includes hooking up, hanging out, drunken make outs, group gatherings, electronic hookups, tagging along, or talking all night at a party or bar*). Why, you ask? Well, there are many reasons, so we'll give you a few: because a date signifies an intent that is clear for both parties; because a date infers that you have a busy and exciting life that would require scheduling to fit someone new in; and how about the best reason of all, which is that **It's Just a F***ing Date** *and you deserve to be asked on one*! Quite honestly, if some guy isn't motivated enough to ask you out, and you've given him the opportunity and encouragement to do so, he doesn't deserve to get to hang out or hook up with you. Simple as that.

We're aware that most of you are less likely to get asked out on a date than asked to hang out. The quasi date is vastly popular with guys for obvious reasons. Hanging out doesn't require an actual plan and is a more nebulous proposition. But with a hang out you don't actually know if you're on a date, and of course there's the possibility that you may end up going "dutch" to said unnamed hang out destination. There may or may not be other people involved in the hang, and it's often at one's house where there's a bedroom nearby, and you know what that means. Actually you don't, because when hanging out leads to having sex you still don't know where you stand. Does it mean that now you're dating because you had sex on your hang out? Or are you now the girl that he gets to have sex with without the pesky process of having to get to know you? Enough already just stop it!

We're not suggesting that you stop living your life spontaneously or veto advances from cute boys, but it's up to you to be clear about the kind of woman you are. The key to finding a great relationship is to stop settling for less. You get to set the value of your time and company—not anybody else— and by participating in less than an actual date you set your value low. The longer you devalue yourself the longer others will too. Here's the wildly obvious secret that you should remind yourself of daily: guys like hanging out, hooking up, getting it on and making out, BUT it means more to them if they have to earn it. That's just part of their nature. Hell, it's a part of human nature!

By partaking in this lame epidemic of Non-Dating, you are positively reinforcing that the lack of effort is good enough for you, that not stepping up to the plate, putting your ass on the line, declaring your attraction and treating a woman right will be greatly rewarded. Constant rewarding for minimal effort over time equals the poor state of dating today. Women are as responsible as men for Non-Dating, and it's time for you to demand more of yourself and the men you choose. This is why we say Don't Settle for Less Than an Actual Date and Stop Selling Yourself Short.

However, because we're realists, we know that a casual invitation to hang out or join a preexisting event is the safest way for a guy to gauge your interest in him. Therefore, we're not going to hold the hard line that says you absolutely under no uncertain circumstances should EVER hang out or join a preplanned event for others if you ARE interested in someone. But what we do say is there's a strategy for how to do it right. You must set limits, be very clear that *it's not a date* and have a clear exit strategy. By setting limits we mean:

1. Make this a one-time thing. You hanging out once is plenty reinforcement that you're interested; the next time he sees you should be when he's asked you on a date.

2. No hanky-panky. Not to be too prudish, but if he gets the prize without the effort he won't make the effort. Yours is an exclusive club and memberships don't come that easily.

3. Leave the room early. The one-time hang out is like a trailer of a movie. This is a preview of all the things they'd get to see if they paid the price of admission, which is asking you out on a date.

Example:

John tells you that he and the guys are meeting over at Skee-lo's Sportatorium to get a few pitchers and watch the World Series and that you should come.

Low Self-Esteem Laura would drop by, drink a few beers, get a buzz on and watch the game, then head off with him for a bite afterwards, then back to his place for a make out party and/or drunken sex.

BUT

A Super Winner Dater Stella might drop by on her way elsewhere, watch the game with John and the guys over a beer, and then when the game is over excuse herself to get back to her previously scheduled plans (and very full life). When asked if she wants to grab a bite, she will flash her flirtiest smile and let him know that she can't tonight, but if he'd like to ask her out to dinner another time she'd love to go on a date with him.

Then, she might give him a little hug or a kiss on the cheek, wave goodbye to his friends and turn on her heel and exit with all eyes on her.

After that kind of exit strategy a rocking lady would be way more likely to get asked out on a date than had she woken up at his house hungover and trying to find her shoes. Look, if you just want to have casual sex or be the kissing bandit when you're hopped up on margaritas, then hooking up, hanging out and quasi dates are fine. But then why are you reading this book? Busted!

The point of this book is to redefine how you date if you're looking for a serious relationship. Rare is the couple that turns the hookup into a fifty-year marriage. Common is the couple that turns the hookup into a six-month relationship that fizzles out because one of them realizes they never really wanted to be in the relationship in the first place. It is the most common outcome of the relationship started from anything other than absolute intention—one realizes that they were never really into it. Let's be honest about these non-dating relationships ... women generally think that if they're agreeable to less than dating and they ride it out that it will eventually lead to something more serious, whereas many guys think that if women are agreeable to less than dating that it's the shortcut to having sex without the responsibility of a relationship. See the difference? So when these relationships, built on an imbalanced foundation of hope for her and sex for him, fall apart it's generally the hopeful party that it really sucks for.

That's why the fourth Super Extraordinary Guideline for Ultra-Successful Winner Dating is Don't Accept Less Than an Actual Date and Stop Selling Yourself Short if what you're looking for is a serious relationship. That means no more hooking up, hanging out and quasi dating. Take a stand and read on, because we're going to show you in the second part of this book how to get guys to ask you out and how to change the way you date. After all, It's Just a F***ing Date and you deserve to be asked out on one!

BUT GREG AND AMIIRA, I HAVE QUESTIONS!

BUT WHAT IF DATING'S TOO MUCH PRESSURE?

Dear Greg and Amiira,

Why can't I just hang out? Why does it have to be so official? It's not the Age of Innocence where you have to marry me before you get in my corset. Hanging out is a much easier way to get to know someone because there's no pressure, where dating is like going on a job interview. Have you seen what the world is like these days? You're sent a group text about where everyone's hooking up, then five drinks later everyone's HOOKING UP! That's the deal.

Amanda
Marina Del Rey, CA

Dear Job Applicant,

While the drunken orgy may seem like the perfect breeding ground for long-lasting love to you, it's not. Look, Ladybug, things don't have to be official if you like things vague or are just looking for a good time at hookup central. But if that's not what you want, you have to ask yourself: Why you don't want to be clear about it? What kind of guy can't handle the pressure of a date? Does he need a cold compress while he lies down from a case of the vapors? Most women think that by asking for some level of certainty about a man's interest, like requiring an actual date, it will scare him off. But to begin editing what you want for fear it might scare someone off or molding yourself into something different to accommodate another's reluctance to step up is a losing and dishonest approach. Look, it makes sense to not run a formal agenda past a person we've just met, but it doesn't make sense to not be clear with yourself about what you want or what you're worth. If a group grope is what you're game for, then that's all you'll get.

Men will be as vague as you let them be, so it's up to you to decide what level of ambiguity works for you.

BUT WHAT IF HE'S TOO SHY TO ASK ME OUT?

Dear Amiira and Greg,

In my circle of friends there's this guy that I've been hanging out with that I really like. His friends tell me he likes me too, but he's really shy and never asks girls out; he just hangs around until the girl makes the first move, then they're boyfriend & girlfriend. Every relationship he's ever had has started like this, so how do you get the shy guy to ask you out when the closest he's ever come is, "Is this seat taken?"

Eden
Dublin, Ireland

Dear Shy By Night,

Oh goodie, the shy guy question! The rules are no different for the shy guy. If he has the ability to be in a relationship with other people, certainly he has the ability to ask you out. Next time he approaches you at friend-fest and asks the magical question, "Is this seat taken?" tell him, "I'm saving it for the guy that's going to ask me out tonight. Is that you?" If he can't manage to nod yes at that, then you have to ask yourself if he's really the kind of guy you envision yourself in a relationship with.

BUT WHAT IF I'VE ALREADY HAD SEX WITH HIM?

Dear Greg and Amiira,

I met this guy at friend's BBQ who was really good looking but not boyfriend material. We flirted the whole time, then ended up hooking up. It was just a sex thing the first couple of times, but now that I know him better I'd really like to date him for real. I've made a few jokes about us going on a date, but he never asks me out; he only offers to bring over a pizza. We obviously get along well, and he knows the sex is good, so why won't he ask me out? Have I blown it?

Ellery
Melbourne, Australia

Dear BBQ-ed,

You never know at first how you're going to feel about someone new, but you do know the difference between thinking you might want to be in a relationship with someone vs. thinking you might want to go skinny-dipping with them. But certainly you have the right to change your mind once you've gotten to know a person. However, by hooking up on day one and positioning it as a casual sleep around thing, you limit the way he perceives you. Guys tend to compartmentalize things, and booty calls and potential girlfriends are two different compartments. The only way to shift gears is to reposition yourself as something other than a booty call. When he calls, you have to be unavailable for a booty call, but offer an opening for on Sunday morning if he'd like to take you to brunch. He won't see you as anything other than the girl he has casual sex with unless you make him. That means that you have to take away the casual sex, and that's generally not a well-received development in the booty call dynamic. It's really hard to go from having sex to holding hands, because once you've had dessert breakfast doesn't seem so appetizing.

WHAT IF IN COLLEGE ALL YOU DID WAS HANG OUT?

Dear Greg and Amiira,

In college there is no real "dating," it's a much more casual process. People hang out in groups in the dorms, pair off, hook up at fraternity parties and generally do everything but date. All my past relationships started that way, and it's hard to really get into the mode of one-on-one dating when it seems almost archaic compared to what's worked for me, what I'm used to, and what's actually happening in the dating world. Why is a real date such a big deal, and how does one make the leap to real dating, let alone get the men to do the same?

Kila

Cambridge, MA

Dear Dorm-ed if you do, Dorm-ed if you don't,

Hey, we went to college, so we get it. But the post-collegiate world calls for you to make some adjustments in your lifestyle. In college you go to keg parties at fraternity houses and wear your pajama bottoms to class, but your boss probably wouldn't think you to be quite an impressive lady if you rocked your PJs to work or showed up at the office party with a beer bong. You adapt to your environment and surroundings so that you can win, and dating is no different. Real dates are a big deal because it lets prospective guys know that your time is precious and you don't have the time to hang out. The message then becomes: "If you want to get involved with me, you've got work on my schedule and within the framework of my life." It puts you in the driver's seat and makes you seem like a huge f***ing prize! Plus, dating can be awesome. And in case they didn't teach you this in college—guys like the girl who is the huge f***ing prize! The how-to is simple, just keep a few key phrases locked and loaded. Like, "If I had time to hang out I'd be spending it with my friends, but I would consider having dinner with you if you want to ask me on a date," or, "Are you asking me on a date? Because I'm not into hanging out, but if this is a date, I'd like to go."

FROM THE OTHER SIDE OF THE FENCE

WHY SHOULD I IF I DON'T HAVE TO?

Dear Greg and Amiira,

Why should I ask girls on a date when I don't have to? Dating cost money and won't get me any more laid than I can already get not dating.

The Anonymous Asshole at the bar down the street,
Your Town

Dear Asshat,

Dude, you shouldn't ask anyone out EVER. Dating is for guys who like women and themselves; clearly you don't. But to be fair, the women who go out with you either A) Just want to get laid (nothing wrong with that) or B) Don't value themselves any more than you do, so it's a perfect match. Asking women out and pursuing them is one of the greatest pleasures in life. Hopefully someday you will meet a girl you really like who you will have to ask out because she accepts no less, and you will come to understand the true pleasure of dating.

THE GUY THAT BLEW IT AND THE CHICK THAT ROCKED IT

I'm all about hooking up or any form of not dating that I can get away with. The only exception to my not dating policy was if there was a dance or function that I needed a date for. Then and only then would I actually call someone in advance and book a date, everything else was as casual as casual gets. You can believe me when I tell you that there are plenty of girls that I could get to hang out any night of the week. Then I met Rebecca at a friend's party. Rebecca was different; she wasn't the most beautiful girl I'd ever seen, but there was something about her. I tried every approach in the book. I talked to her, flirted with her, offered to drive her home, walk her home, take her home, get her a drink, take her outside for some "air", see if she wanted to hit another party, everything. She was nice, she was confident and she was definitely out of my league. Nothing happened that night or the next few times we were at the same parties. Finally I asked her what I had to do to spend some time with her. Her answer was, "You'd have to ask me out on a date." Here's where I blew it—I asked her back, "What kind of date?" She laughed and said, "It's not going to work. You're just a boy and I date men." I must have tried a dozen times after that to ask her on a date, but she never would go out with me. Then I met her new boyfriend and I asked him, "How'd you get Rebecca to go out with you?" Get this, he said, "I asked her out." I still keep things casual with most girls, but when I meet one that I might really like ... I don't even try to get her to hang out with me, I just straight up ask her on a date. Know what? Asking a girl out on a date actually makes me feel like more of a George Clooney kind of super suave kind of guy. Like I'm the shit. I don't know why but it just does.

Partick

Newark, NJ

IT WORKED FOR ME!

For years I've been the most accommodating and least demanding potential date for every guy I've shared a decent conversation, drunken kiss or romp in the hay with. I've always thought if I wanted to actually be taken on a date instead of just hanging out that guys would think I was high maintenance and not want to be with me. So basically I was agreeable to all forms of not dating. None of these "relationships" (and I use that term very loosely) ever lasted very long, and a lot of times I was the only one that even thought it as sort of a relationship. I was starting to feel really crappy about men and myself, plus I was at the point where I was wondering what was wrong with me. I hadn't been asked on a date in over six years. Then I met this guy I really liked who had a girlfriend, so obviously I didn't do anything other than talk to him the few times we came across each other. But I always thought that he was the kind of guy I'd like to go out with. Cut to six months later after I've taken a vow in front of my best friend and a Cadillac Margarita that from now on I'm *only* going out on dates—I run into him. After catching up and finding that he and his girlfriend are no longer, he says that we should hang out some time. The old me would have agreed and hoped he even remembered to text me, but the new improved vow-in-front-of-a-Cadillac-Margarita me said, "I'm not really a hanger outer. But I bet if you asked me on a date I'd say, 'Yes.'" Not only did I completely surprise myself with how ballsy I was, but for the first time in six years I felt really good about myself. And you know what? He asked me out right there on the spot, told me he liked my confidence, and has continued to ask me out for the last three months. So I'm here to say that being the kind of gal that doesn't accept less than a date really works!

Kristie

Taos, NM

FIRST PERSON SINGLE, BY AMIIRA

I used to like hanging out with guys because it seemed so much easier and less formal than dating … except when I really liked someone and realized that it's not easy at all. In fact, it's completely consuming with the whole fuzzy nebulous "what are we doing, how can I turn this into a date, and how can I tell if he really likes me?" thoughts that overtake your brain. It's having enough of those experiences and also, if I'm being honest, reaching a level of maturity that makes you not like hanging out any more. Or at least that's how it was for me. Many of my relationships started as hanging out then became something more, but I have to be clear that I was kind of a prudish hang. I didn't do a lot of messing around or sleeping around. I wasn't a girl you were going to score with easily because I had downed a few glasses of pinot grigio because even drunk I would rather talk to a cute boy about his record collection than have my tongue down his throat. I don't know why that is, and certainly there are some boys that I should have had sex with. But as I got older and became clearer about who I was and what kind of people I wanted in my life— be it friends, business associates or boyfriends—I found myself detaching from people that were cloudy about their lives. It's almost a cliché, but some days you just wake up and don't want your relationships to be so difficult, delicate or tenuous. In this period of moving through life with real direction and clarity, an interesting thing happened. I started getting asked out on dates by guys that had their shit together as well as being asked to hang out by guys that had girlfriends, local bands, no ambition and bad reputations. So I went on actual dates and declined the hang out invitations. A funny thing happened then … the hang outers started asking me on dates too when I wouldn't hang out with them. I had a dating renaissance and it rocked. Not because every date was spectacular or even good, but because I was clear about what his and my intentions both were when going on the date. Clarity about who I am, how valuable my time is and how I date became my compass and ultimately led me to the right man for me.

THOUGHTS FROM MAN CITY

I don't speak for all men; I can only speak for myself and about the conversations I've had with my buddies. My experience was always that if I didn't have to put a name on it, I didn't. Meaning if a lady would let me just hang out or drop by or rock the booty call, I would. If I could just meet her out with her friends, have a couple of drinks and go back to her place, that was great. But it was *never* something I was serious about. Then if she happened to mention to someone who we were dating, I would always be surprised because I thought that we were just hanging out, WHICH IS NOT DATING. Dating to me has always implied seriousness and intent to pursue a relationship. It only really happened when I was really taken with someone so much so that I was willing to work for it. However, I was on the opposite side of it as well, where I was with a girl who really never wanted to do anything but hang out and have sex. Sounds ideal, right? It would have been if I hadn't liked her so much and wanted more. Here's the truth about Men: Men want to have relationships too, and when we do, we act like it and ask you on dates.

DATING FORTUNE COOKIE

You determine your worth. If a non-date is what you will settle for then a non-date is all you will get.

WORST DATE EVER

I met this totally awesome guy while I was interning at a law firm in San Francisco. He was this hot blond bartender named Taylor that worked at the yuppie pub down the street from my office. I worked long hours and usually stopped in to say "Hi" during last call. I could tell he liked me because I don't think I paid for a drink but maybe one time. Sometimes I would hang out with him and the rest of the bar staff after closing hours, and we'd usually end up making out. After about a month of this, I remember thinking how awesome it was to kind of have a boyfriend. I finally got hired at the law firm full-time and I was wanted to take Taylor out to celebrate. I made reservations at a great restaurant, surprised him at work and took him out to blow my first paycheck. At dinner I told him my news and that I wanted to celebrate with the guy I'm dating. He stopped me dead in my tracks and said, "Wait a minute. We're not dating because I've never asked you on a date." I thought he was being playful so I batted my eyes and asked him if he'd like to ask me on an official date, and he said, "Not really. I only ask girls out that I really like." I was stunned. So I asked him what that made me and he told me, "I don't know, a girl that let's me feel her up in the bathroom."

IT'S JUST A F***ING DATE PT. 1

What's the big deal? It's not like you are being unreasonable. It's a date. And don't you deserve to go on one? Our answer is yes. If he can't muster up the energy or the imagination to at least take you to coffee then he's not available to receive a membership to Club You. The philosophy of this book is simple: going on the actual date shouldn't be such a big deal, but getting to go out with you sure as heck is. So set your standards to "DATE" mode and rock the house.

THE ORIGINAL WORLD FAMOUS WINNER DATER'S WORKBOOK

Congratulations! You are no longer a person that just lets dating happen to them. You are in the driver's seat and today is the day that you are finally on your way. Mark it in your journals; this is the first day of your New Dating Policy! "Dating policy? Journals? C'mon. You don't really expect me to write a dating policy, do you? I thought you guys were the anti-self-help, self-help guys?" Kiddo, you can do whatever you want, but we found, as many others have, that it really makes a difference when you plot your own course on paper. It gives you something tangible to remind yourself of who you are trying to be and how you want to honor yourself on those days you can't remember or want to cave on the standards you've set for yourself because it seems too hard. Plus, we just bought a lot of stock in notepad company and are hoping to make a killing. Need some help? Read the sample below and then create you own using the words you like.

> I, ***your name here***, am a person who goes out on dates. If I like someone and I think there may be a chance that I might really want to be with them, then I will take the time to get to know them by dating them. I don't give my time away because it is precious. I don't hang out, hook up, accept electronic dating substitutes or compromise what's important to me. This makes me a sexier and more interesting person because I know my value and it is sky-high, motherf***ers!!!!

Okay, you get the idea, so give it a try. Ready, steady, go!

next. Abracadabra! You're playing emotional chess (which is a bad dating game) and trying to force someone to either "mate" you or retreat. Once you're in that mode you're not even really dating each other any more. You're dating the version of the person that's under pressure to figure out how they truly feel at an accelerated pace. They're dating the version of you that you're pretending to be to make them feel the things you want them to feel in order to commit to you. Ultimately it's a mess because neither of you are actually genuinely being yourselves nor are you experiencing your emotional responses in an organic nature or at the pace that is right for you as individuals. Next thing you know you've become a crazy person.

If you take just one piece of advice from us let it be this: needing constant reassurance manifests itself in ways that will surely cause the person you're newly dating to think you are an insecure freak and depart your company quickly. YOU MUST SHOW SOME RESTRAINT. Under no circumstances is it a good idea to plan the wedding after the 1st date, call him twenty times a day, analyze the relationship nonstop, or be desperate for definition before you know their middle name, because that's what a crazy person does. Even when you think you have your need in check, it is often subconsciously motivating us to act on an impulse. That's why you have to actually work diligently at all times. Like, say you're on a date and you have an uncontrollable urge to for him to reassure you that you're pretty … instead of fishing for the compliment, stuff your mouth with pats of butter, breadsticks or your napkin until the urge passes. Run to the bathroom and splash cold water on your face, then lock yourself in a stall until you can resist, or borrow his phone and excuse yourself to make an important phone call to yourself, then leave yourself a voicemail on your mobile phone begging you not to blow it. That way you can recheck that message all night long if you need to. See how there are solutions right in front of your face? Only you can stop the crazy, needy girl in your head.

We know that you don't want to play games when dating, but there is a very important game to be played and it's called **Don't Freak People Out With Your Need.** It's not a

game of tactics and deception (like waiting two or three
to call back and pretending to have gotten busy), or "how
I be different so I can trick them into liking me?" or "how can
I manipulate this person into loving me?" Those of you who
refuse to acknowledge that there is a *right* game to be played are
the least likely to succeed because you're actually playing another
game called "*I'm ignoring the rules of engagement and I don't care what
you think or feel about it.*"

Love feels unlike anything else on this planet, with the
small exception of the Cadbury Creme Egg. It is glorious,
magnificent and reassuring. Love makes you feel confident and
powerful, secure in your place in this world. The road to love
feels considerably less good than that as it is paved with fear
of getting hurt and "what if he doesn't like me, like me?" It's
unknown territory and thusly you want constant around-the-
clock reassurances that you're going in the right direction and
that everything is going to be okay. You want to define things,
know where you stand, know how much they like you and
whether or not this is going to be the one. You find yourself
wanting to call the person regardless of the fact that you've only
gone out with them twice (three times if you count meeting him
and his buddies at the beer garden) and say, "Hey, is this going
to happen or not? 'Cause I'm losing my shit over here." Even
though the rational part of you knows that asking for definition
this early in the relationship will backfire, you can't help
yourself. Our insecurities manifest the most difficult emotions
to manage, so people get caught up in the result rather than
in building the relationship. The need for definition overrides
better judgment—it's the biggest pitfall for today's Daters.

This method of dating is backwards. As opposed to figuring
out "how can I get you to love me?" you should be thinking:
"How about if I take a moment to actually see where I am with
this and do I even like you?" That's a completely different mindset
that implements a much different and healthy dating strategy.

A relationship is an evolution, and it's much more enjoyable
if you're actually experiencing it instead of just trying to get to
the finish line. Sometimes the mind is no match for the feelings

that rule us. So take a deep breath and get a handle on your bad self. Patience, young grasshopper.

BUT GREG AND AMIIRA, I HAVE QUESTIONS!

BUT WHAT IF I NEED TO KNOW WHERE "IT'S" GOING BECAUSE I HAVE TO RSVP FOR A WEDDING?

Dear Greg and Amiira,

What's up with guys? This guy asked me out last year when I had a boyfriend, so I politely declined, but he kept emailing me occasionally to let me know that if I ever was single that he wanted the first date. So I'm finally single and we go out on a great date. He says it was completely worth the wait, and we make plans for another. After a few more dates I asked him if he'll go to my cousin's wedding with me in two months (I have to send in the response card that far ahead because apparently it's of national importance that I reserve the correct number of dinners) and he goes completely strange on me. Granted, him agreeing would presume that we'll be going out two months from now, but if it's already going so well and he waited for a whole year to go out with me in the first place, why's that such a stretch?

Sienna

Birmingham, England

Dear Houdini,

Ahhhh, the old wedding date trick. This one's been going around for decades, and yet every woman we've ever talked to thinks she's the first one to find the loophole to locking down a relationship. It doesn't matter if it's your cousin's wedding, a trip to the Super Bowl, tea with the Queen or tickets to the Academy Awards—you can't bribe or coerce someone into a committed relationship and expect a good result. Dudes get freaked out when you try to rush them because it makes you seem needy and panicky. If you think you're not putting pressure on the other person because "it's no big deal" then you're just playing a game with yourself. If you were really confident in the future of the relationship you'd RSVP for two and invite them when it's closer to the actual wedding. And if they're not in the picture any more then you take a friend who's happy to go since you didn't dump them for the bozo that dumped you before your cousin's wedding. A general rule is no locking down future plans until you've been together for an amount of time greater than the distance between now and the upcoming event and a minimum of two months. A cousin's wedding ... really?

WHY DOES IT FREAK HIM OUT THAT WE'RE PERFECT FOR EACH OTHER?

Dear Greg and Amiira,

My friend Belinda set me up with her older brother Ryan because she thought we'd have so much in common. So Ryan and I decided to go out for Indian food and to see Amy Winehouse, who we had discovered we both totally loved. Dinner was great, our conversation couldn't have clicked any better, and we have absolutely everything in common. We even joked about getting married because it was weird how completely alike we are and how well our date was going. The concert was amazing and by the end of it he was standing behind me with his arms wrapped tightly around me like I was his girl. We made out in his car for an hour, and it was the best date I ever had, so I fully expected that we we're kind of going out (what with the wedding comment over dinner) and made some kind of joke about how when we get hitched I'm going to make both he and Belinda take my surname instead of taking theirs. The next day I called him and he was totally a different guy—really acting distant and non-committal about getting together. So I called Belinda to see if he had reported back to her after our date, and she told me that he said that I was a little too excited about the marriage idea and it made me seem desperate for a boyfriend. Can you believe that? We had the best date ever; he even said that we're perfect for each other, so I was excited by that, but desperate? C'mon. What I can do to make him think I'm not desperate so he'll go out with me again?

Tabitha
Leeds, England

Desperately Seeking Tabitha,

Look, we weren't there and we didn't hear the joke, but we have to say that the word married is a loaded gun on the first date. Even if you meant it to be a pop gun and he mistook it for an Uzi. At some point in the midst of the world's best first date he took the marriage joke to heart and either sensed some real desperation, projected some desperation as an excuse to bail, or maybe he scares easily. Or it could be that you are perfect for him and he's not ready to settle down, so he's blowing you off and making you the fall guy. Dudes panic when things are going too well too soon; they think that there must be something wrong that they can't see. In any case this guy and you weren't as ideal a match as you had thought because if the date was as stellar as you say, he wouldn't have let a joke keep him from seeing you again. Sorry, sweet potato, but you'd best move on and next time keep all marriage jokes under wraps until you're with your fiancé because dudes are easily freaked by marriage. By the way, consider yourself blessed to have gotten to see Amy Winehouse. That's something most of us never got to experience.

WHAT IF I WASN'T NEEDY THEN BUT I'M FEELING IT NOW?

Dear Amiira and Greggers,

Grant and I have been dating for about four months, and though things are going really well, I'm concerned. See, he was very clear up front about not wanting a serious relationship and feeling like he didn't want to be responsible for someone else, so I played it all casual and cool at the beginning. Not really caring about how often we saw each other or what our status as a couple was (or at least I pretended to). I didn't act needy or insecure at all; I was completely nonchalant about the whole thing. Then when he was enjoying the benefits of our casual and uncomplicated dating, I started slowly moving a few of my things into his place. I took over a drawer for undergarments and reserve clothing in case I stayed over, put some of my toiletries in his medicine cabinet and started to stock the fridge with my brand of yogurt and breakfast foods, and I made myself a key to his place under the guise of being able to walk and feed his dog when he has to work late. I just kind of started staying over a few times a week to the point where we have become boyfriend/girlfriend, or at least I assume we are because I've made it kind of impossible for him to date anyone else. Now he seems to be pulling back from me a little, acting differently and getting really irritated with me. I think I'm in love with him and I'm afraid he thinks I tricked him into being my boyfriend and is reconsidering being with me. I can't seem to stop asking him for reassurance that we're good and I feel all panicky. What do I do?

    Petra

    Ottawa, Canada

Dear Sneaky Pete,

    It sounds like you did trick him into being your boyfriend. He was clear with you at the beginning about not wanting a serious relationship, and then you disregarded his feelings and moved yourself in. We can't say this enough—people get to their feelings at their own pace. So even if you manipulate someone into committing to something faster than he wanted to so that you could have what you wanted, you're screwed. Because you know that at the bottom of his heart he has doubts because he wasn't true to his inner emotional clock, he's not comfortable with what you need from him and you've tricked him into being in this relationship. So great, now you will always be wondering if he's going to change his mind because of that doubt, or worse, look for something better. If you thought you needed reassurance before you were boyfriend and girlfriend, how's it going to feel now that the stakes are higher and you have to worry every time he leaves the house that he'll realize he doesn't want to be with you? Need is a dangerous thing to be in servitude, to and it can make you crazy. You should be honest with your dude, tell him that you may have rushed him into this and are happy to back off and give him some space if he needs it to figure out his feelings. Regardless of how things shake down, this way as least you still have your dignity, which is more than many ladies have during their relationship reckoning.

IS THERE A DIFFERENCE BETWEEN BEING NEEDY AND BEING HONEST?

Dear Greg and Amiira,

    I was on a first date with this new guy and it was going really well. We talked really easily, there was never a lull, and he's really gorgeous. Here's where things go from well to not so well. I got a bit tipsy and laid my cards on the table and said something like, "I don't play games, this is who I am.

I'm not going to pretend I don't like you so that you'll like me more. I like you a lot and think we'd be great together." I thought a guy like John would appreciate my honesty, but that wasn't his reaction. He was like, "This is just a first date. I don't even know you yet, and I certainly can't tell you that we're going to have a future together. Let's just see how we get through dinner because I'm not really ready to get tied down before dessert." I totally blew it and he never called again. I thought being honest was a good thing; what did I do wrong?

> *Kristen*
> *Sydney, Australia*

Dear Tipsy Roulette,

Being honest is a good thing, so let us be honest with you. What a bozo move that was! Before you are honest with someone else it's imperative that you be honest with yourself. You should have asked yourself, "Why do I need to know where this is going right now?" Or how about: "Is this person really ready for me to lay all my cards on the table right now?" Or: "Do I want to ruin the good feelings I'm having and the ones he's having by trying to solidify an answer about the future?" or "Can't I wait until at least the end of the third date?" Or even: "Do I want to appear completely crazy?" Once you've answered these maybe you'll feel differently about being so honest. Look, Kristen, using honesty as a reason to actually push someone away is a neat trick because then you can pretend he's the bad guy. But there are better ways to push someone away and not get what you want. Hey, go easy in the drinks next time; they're not helping.

FROM THE OTHER SIDE OF THE FENCE

HOW DO I MAKE SOMEONE BACK OFF A BIT SO THEY DON'T WRECK IT?

Dear Greg and Amiira,

I started dating a girl I met on the subway one afternoon, which seemed like a massive stroke of good luck at first. The thing is that after a couple of dates she started waiting for me on the subway platform so we could ride together everyday. I know I should think it's nice, but it feels claustrophobic, like I'm supposed to see her every day now. She doesn't say that, but it's weird to ride home everyday after work and have the "what are you doing for dinner conversation" and not feel like she's waiting for me to ask her out. I can't tell whether she has no life or just digs me a lot, but either way it's more than I bargained for and it's freaking me out. How do I get her to back it up a bit?

Marcus
New York, NY

Dear Subwait,

Wow. This is a tough one. It's almost like you want to shout to her: "No, wait, don't ruin this." She probably has no idea that she is ruining it, either. This is an example of freaking people out with your need and being too available. Even if she's not necessarily a needy person she's making you think she's got nothing better to do than wait around for you at the subway. While that should be flattering, let's be real—it's a colossal turnoff. If she had done it once and surprised you, you would have been rocked by it, but by day five it's feeling more like stalker than rocker. If you really like her, you should just tell her what's up. Try something like: "The *He's Just Not That Into You* guys told me that you'd appreciate my honesty so here goes … I like you but I can't decide if I really like you because I see you too often. I need to not see you so that I can think about you and hopefully miss you waiting for me at the subway." Then jam your hands in your pockets and look at your shoes—girls love that. It makes you look vulnerable and boyish when you do that, and it'll soften the blow and make it seem like it's your own deal, not something she should be embarrassed about.

THE CHICK THAT BLEW IT

Why is it that every time I start dating a girl I like she turns into someone I can't deal with at the six-week mark? It's the same thing almost every time: it starts off great, we get along great, we're taking our time getting to know each other, then six weeks into it she starts her descent into becoming the weirdly insecure version of herself. I know it has everything to do with the fact that I have to travel every two months for work, so it never fails that I have to go out of town just when we're hitting our stride. I always make it a point to reassure her that I will call when I can but that I can't always talk during the day. I always send flowers with a note saying that I'll miss her. So when I started dating Ivy I was totally upfront about what has happened in the past, and she swore that she was not like that at all. So I went away, like I told her I would have to do for work, and I couldn't call as much. At first it seemed okay, but by the fifth day everything changed; instead of hearing, "Hey!" when I called I got the icy, "How nice of you to take time out of your busy schedule to call me." Or if I called to say goodnight, it's like thirty minutes of having to assure her that I miss her and am thinking about her. Jesus! If I wasn't thinking about her I wouldn't have called and now all I'm thinking is that I wish I hadn't called. Then there's the "Do U still miss me?" texts, "Just thinking about you" emails and the "Give me a call when you get a chance" voicemails that distract me from my work and make me feel guilty and kind of annoyed, if I'm being honest. When I'm on a business trip I'm generally with my boss, who is a very serious business man, or with clients that don't love me taking time out to address my personal life. By the time I'm supposed to come home I don't feel the same way I did about her before I left because I've been driven crazy by a woman who either thinks I'm going to cheat on her or forget she exists. Then I'm the bad guy because she doesn't believe that I like her enough, and instead of this being a great opportunity for me to miss her I'm completely irritated by her and then I can't get back to liking her again.

Tommy
Calabasas, CA

MAYBE YOU GUYS ARE RIGHT

I know that I can get insecure and needy when I like someone a lot and I'm not getting the total reinforcement that we're going to be together next month or next year. I can feel my uneasiness rising every time we are apart and I haven't heard from him in a day. A day seems like an eternity when you like someone too much and can't tell if they're just dipping their toes in the pool or jumping in with both feet. I've always been the type of person that likes someone too much too fast then wrecks it by scaring him off by needing to know what's going to happen next. It's only after the deed is done that I can see how totally desperate I must seem to them trying to turn a third date into a committed relationship. It's embarrassing to look back at some of the things I've done. So now that I'm thirty I've decided that I am no longer allowing myself to act on my needy impulses when dealing with a new guy. The rule is if you haven't made me your girlfriend, I am not going to be your problem. I can handle myself. Now that's all easier said than done, and of course as soon as I made this declaration I met Bryan. But this time I was determined to keep my self-destructive impulses under control, so any time I was feeling insecure and wanting to fish for reassurance I called my friends and had them talk me out of reaching out to him. Instead they sang my praises and kept reminding me that I would feel and be ten times more attractive if I just managed to keep my sanity. So Bryan and I are going on six months together, and even though I had crazy feelings I never exposed them to him. Not only has told me that the thing he loves most about me is that I'm the most independent and together woman he's ever dated, but he's also shared past horror stories of women pressuring him and being need freaks. (Some of whose actions I totally have been guilty of in the past! Shhhh!) Not only do I feel like a new person for conquering my need, but I also *finally* got the guy!

Janessa

Chicago, IL

FIRST PERSON SINGLE, BY AMIIRA

I have felt both the crushing need of another and been the crusher myself. Neither of those experiences are ones I'd like to revisit for any number of reasons. From what I can gather from my experiences there seems to be this invisible thread that connects Need with Respect. Or rather, the way someone handles their own need is directly proportional to how much respect they command from the person that they need so desperately from. You can't always muster up respect when dignity has left the building and desperation has surfaced in its place. It's hard to feel good about someone whose sudden panic has shattered their normal cool exterior and turned them into a Clinger. We've all been there to some degree or another when the person you're *kind of* going out with has that seismic shift and suddenly can't bear the idea of continuing in the ambiguity that is supposed to be dating for one moment longer. So they stick to you like glue, or worse yet, check up on you, constantly making jokes about the future and fishing for assurance that you are on your way to being serious about them. It's the worst! I remember really liking a guy I had been seeing for a few weeks only to be completely turned off when his easygoing nature was overtaken by a sudden need to lock down our relationship. The constant having to talk about a future that I could not see coupled with his omnipresence was suffocating and ultimately the beginning of the end. Even worse is the knowledge that I've been the needy one before, seeking validation and reassurance from someone who shrinks from you the more you persist. Even fifteen years later I can still recall how sucky it felt to be so weak and out of control of my own emotions and behaviors. We all learn from our mistakes; that's why they say that hindsight is 20/20. So remember that the goal is to keep your self-respect above all and be someone who he will want to run *to*, not run *from*.

THOUGHTS FROM MAN CITY

Look, it's pretty simple: guys don't like to be rushed into committing to anything bigger than what is for lunch. We especially don't like to be rushed when dating, because when you rush us you've basically folded your cards and said, "I'm yours for the taking," and the chase is over. When you rush us into reassuring you that we like you, the flattery you want us to feel is completely drowned out by the hydraulics of the truck that's about to dump a pile of emotional responsibility into our laps. When you rush us, things go all snowy and weird in our heads and the girl you couldn't wait to get undressed becomes the girl with an alarming amount of need. Even if you're not that, it's the panicked place that we go to in record time. The thing is we want to know you are busy and we'd be lucky to get to see you, so when you are willing to drop everything for us this early in the game we panic. We panic because it feels like suddenly we have to take care of you or that you are looking to us to make you happy, and we don't know how to do that. That may not be your truth; you might just be excited and forthcoming with your feelings, but that's how we react. Here's the thing: once someone rushes you or has needs that you aren't sure you can handle, it makes you feel differently about them. You can go from worshipping someone to being completely unsure about that same person in the time it takes to say, "So are we boyfriend/girlfriend or what?" If you don't have a visual for what need feels like, it's like someone pulling your pant leg when you are drowning, and it's scary to men. Yes, we know that you've been there too, but it's not like you ladies love the needy guy. Human beings don't like to be rushed up on; it's just how we are. It's not something that can be changed; it's a survival instinct. Hell, even dogs circle around each other a few times before they sniff butts. Now isn't that sexy?

DATING FORTUNE COOKIE

*The only thing less sexy than overwhelming need
is shitting your pants.*

WORST DATE EVER

I was on a date with a girl from work; we got along great on the job and as she was leaving to pursue another career so I felt free to ask her out. We went to dinner at a Comedy Club. We got along okay, but thank God there was someone else doing the talking. We were chatting and laughing, but she seemed distracted and she kept looking back over her shoulder. Then finally she literally shouted, "If you are going to look at other f***ing women all night then why don't you take me home!" Seriously, I was shocked. Hey, I'm no saint; I've looked at other women before when on a date, but even when I did I was pretty discreet. But that night I wasn't looking at other women, in fact I was pretty interested in my date and actually remember that I was trying to make sure I was making eye contact as much as possible. So I said as much, and she paused a moment and then said, "See you're doing it again." She slammed down her fork and that's when I realized she was referring to my Amblyopia, or "lazy eye." Well, needless to say she was pretty embarrassed when I explained myself. She apologized and we had an okay time. I never asked her out again, partly because I don't like yellers, but mostly because that date was such a tour of her insecurities. I was completely attuned to my date, and regardless of my body language or comments about how great she was, all she was concerned about was that there was an imaginary girl over her shoulder that was prettier and better than she was. I can only imagine if she needed that much reassurance during dinner what dating her further would be like. Plus, I had my lazy eye at work, which she would have easily noticed had she paid as much attention to me then in broad daylight as she did in the dim corners of a Comedy Club.

HE'S JUST A F***ING GUY

C'mon now. He's just a guy. That's it. And you don't need a guy to make you happy. Sure, it's great to share your awesomeness with someone, but not any guy will do for you and in fact most of them won't. You are selective because you are not needy and because you are not needy, you get to decide who's lucky enough to take the ride with you. After all, it's just a guy; it's not like it's cake.

THE ORIGINAL WORLD FAMOUS WINNER DATER'S WORKBOOK

It's time to take control of yourself so that from now on you can be self-possessed when you're dating. To do that we must figure out what you're afraid of and why your need to know what someone else is thinking, feeling and doing is getting the best of you. We'd like you to do some reflecting and really think about these questions before you answer them.

When you like a guy, what do you feel?

At what point do your feelings of liking him make you more uncomfortable than excited?

What feels better: the anxiety of a "where's this thing going?" conversation or meeting your girlfriends for a pedicure?

Is it better to take your time figuring out what to order off of a new menu or be rushed by a passively impatient waiter? Why?

Is it better to try on a pair of shoes that you're going to wear a lot to see if they fit and are comfortable or just plop down your cash and hope they don't make your feet sweat or give you blisters?

If the guy that you like doesn't like you back do you:
a) Die of heart failure?
b) Turn to a life of crime on the streets?
c) Set his car on fire and spend sixty days in prison?
d) Be disappointed but get over it the next time a cute boy looks your way?

Would you rather go out with someone who's kind of into you or be single and still be looking for the guy that's totally into you? Why?

How much does it matter what he's thinking or feeling?

If he doesn't like you are you not a good person?

If he doesn't like you will you never have another chance of finding someone?

If he doesn't like you do you really want to go out with him?

Now write the following one hundred times on a chalkboard:

"I will not be needy or a crazy person. I will concentrate on how *I* feel because that is what's important."

Look, most guys you go out with aren't going to be the guy for you. It's just the way life works, that we like many but only choose one. So you must understand that the *right* relationship is what you're trying to find and the *right* relationship won't make you a crazy needy person. So when you're having those dreaded feelings of need and insecurity they should be your first clue that this is probably not the guy for you because *HE* wouldn't want you to feel that way.

PRINCIPLE #6
DOORMATS FINISH LAST
AND END UP IN THE DIRT

Setting Up Some Standards and Losing the Deal Breakers

Many people go through their lives setting unnecessary deal breakers that ultimately keep them from succeeding in the areas that they want success in the most. And yet they're the last people to see it, much less admit to it. They're the people that proclaim things like: "He's got to be taller than me and own his own home or I'm not interested." Really? Why is that? Because you're insecure about being seen with someone shorter than you? You sound really deep. Why can't he move into your home if things get serious? Oh right, you probably don't own one. That seems fair.

The deal breaker types are those that create a list of things that they want (and don't want) out of a mate, then set parameters that someone must fall within in order to have real potential as a partner. This sounds like a good idea in concept; certainly it's better than having no idea at all about what you want or just playing drunken roulette and grabbing the first person you see at the "Lion's Den Bar & Grill Happy Hour and Hot Wing Ding" in hopes that it'll pan out and become a relationship. The problem with the *idea* of deal breakers is that *by setting them you are working against the very properties and nature of a great relationship* instead of encouraging one. **Setting parameters to determine someone's worth or viability as a romantic partner assumes that they don't have other areas of value**

that could possibly be more appealing than the ideas or wants that YOU have. It also assumes that how they are in this moment in time is all they will ever be. What if the love of your life turns out to be a social worker who fights for the rights of children and raises loads of money for worthwhile charities but doesn't have much more than the shirt on his back and rents a tiny flat? You know Bill Gates wasn't always as wealthy as Bill Gates and Ryan Gosling wasn't always as hot as Ryan Gosling. Something to have a think about.

THE BIG DIFFERENCE BETWEEN STANDARDS AND DEAL BREAKERS

There's a difference between having standards and having deal breakers when dating, though many think they are the same thing. Having standards is completely different. "How?" We're glad you asked.

> *Standards* are about how YOU LIVE YOUR LIFE, where Deal Breakers are about how YOU VIEW THEIRS.

> *Standards* are you living your life at a higher level and only accepting things that strive for excellence—it's living a life of quality choices and high self worth.

> *Deal Breakers* are you QUANTIFYING another person's assets or attributes to validate your worth.

> *Standards* are not about hair color or record collections, height or financial worth. They are about tolerable behaviors, about the kind of relationship you want to be in and the way you want to be treated

> *Standards* are you walking the walk. Deal Breakers are you talking the talk.

Standards are defined as a level of quality or excellence that is accepted as the norm or by which actual attainments are judged. It's about how you live. Having a set list of personal Deal Breakers seems like a surefire way to save you from winding up in a bum relationship. However, the truth is that most of those people end up being either eternally single or "settling" for someone who they consider to be less than what they wanted in a mate. And how great for the person that they "settled" for—a relationship based on the thought that they, as a partner and a person, are better than nothing but still not as good as themselves. That must feel good for both parties. What a great story to tell your kids. The bottom line is that most Deal Breakers are unnecessary requirements that you've set to validate you and really don't have much to do with the other person. If a relationship is good and worthwhile, the things you want will work themselves out anyway.

Still confused about the difference? Maybe this will help …

> **Standard:** I don't date people that drink so excessively that it makes me uncomfortable.

> **Deal Breaker:** I don't date people that drink blue fruity drinks.

> **Standard:** I won't date men who consistently don't do what they say they're going to do.

> **Deal Breaker:** If he forgets to call me one time he's done.

> **Standard:** I won't date anyone who's emotionally unavailable.

> **Deal Breaker:** I won't date anyone less than six feet tall.

Get it now? Standards are a level by which you live or, in this case specifically, date, and on which you will not compromise. "How is that not a deal breaker?" you ask. Because they are not about aesthetics and material value; they are about *tolerable behaviors, about the kind of relationship you want to be in and the way you want to be treated.* Living with a set of standards tells the world "this is how I operate." Deal breakers tell the world "these are my requirements." People automatically assume that they already live by a solid set of standards, and in truth they probably do … except when it comes to dating. For some reason when it comes to dating people compromise their standards in hopes that they will get something lasting in return. Don't you want your relationship to be of the highest quality? Shouldn't the person you share your life with and the relationship that you turn to in your best and worst times be of the highest standards?

Living and dating with standards means holding yourself and those around you to behavior that honors a higher caliber of life (and we're not talking about material things) … it also weeds out the riffraff, so you really can't argue with us on this one. If you want a relationship with someone who honors and respects you and that you honor and respect, you must operate at a level worthy of such things. How do you do that? Well, let's think about it.

You will need to be …

Someone who values himself or herself as much as they value the person they want to be with. *('Cause who's the awesome catch that wants to get saddled with "Grabby can't let go," a needy partner that doesn't feel worthy of them?)*

Someone who is considerate and generous but expects consideration and generosity in return. *(As in I scratch your back you run to market at 4:00 a.m. for a pint of dulce de leche)*

Someone who is respectful and honest to others and accepts no less from others. *(C'mon, this* *one's obvious, right? It's not? Man, are you in trouble.)*

Someone who has a sense of purpose and attracts others who have purpose, not dead weight and codependents. *(Coffee is for closers. See the movie* Glengarry Glen Ross *for more on this … or don't. Just find a person with a sense of purpose and you'll see what we mean. You will find them in the super successful winner department of your local grocery store.)*

Someone who surrounds himself or herself with excellence that honors their worth, be it a clean house, a well-groomed appearance or a coterie of good friends. *(Did you notice we didn't say a jobless slob with a Barbie doll head collection? Did we knock your socks off with the use of coterie?)*

Someone who elicits respect and doesn't endure those who aren't respectful, be it a date, a boss, a friend or a family member. Doormats finish last and end up in the dirt. *(Sad but true, ask your doormat. By the way, if you have a doormat you already are on your way to becoming a person who honors themselves.)*

Think of what you stand for in life, what you represent in the world, how your friendships exist, and what you want out of a relationship. Then know that the exceptions and excuses you make for people by lowering your standards will only bite you in the ass later. We know it from experience and we've got the bite marks to prove it.

BUT GREG AND AMIIRA, I HAVE QUESTIONS!

BUT WHAT IF I KNOW WHAT I WANT REGARDLESS OF WHAT YOU CALL IT?

Dear Greg and Amiira,

*   I know what I want out of life and a relationship and it's not*

negotiable. So when I'm on a first date I cut to the chase and tell the guy what I'm looking for—what my criteria is (i.e. must love travel, wants to get married, has to love cats, etc.) so that we don't waste a lot of time if we're not going to be compatible. I don't play games and some guys find my honesty off-putting, but others are grateful for it and glad for the time I saved them. My girlfriends think I'm crazy and am ruining my chances of getting asked out on a second date; I think I'm saving myself from the heartache of getting attached to someone who doesn't share your goals. What do you think?

Loz
Manchester, England

Dear Must Love Cats,

I think that's a great idea. I actually think you should also get a credit report, a field sobriety test, and ask for three references not including family. While you are at it, why don't you bring your cat on the date so that you can appear totally crazy and never end up with anyone except Whiskers. Look, I know it seems like you are trying to be smart about it, but what you are actually doing is driving people away and limiting your perception of yourself and any potential suitor to who they are today. You actually ARE playing a game; it's a game called "How Can I Keep Myself from Being Vulnerable to Getting Hurt?" When you meet someone of quality that has their own interests, who's to say that that wouldn't expand YOUR interests or vice versa? The thing you're not taking into account is that people evolve when they come together if it's a good match, and when you cut someone off at the knees by limiting them to your narrow-minded version of suitability YOU'RE THE ONE WHO'S BLOWING IT. because they'll go on to find someone else that's more flexible and adventurous to evolve with while you stay lonely but protected. Besides, cutting someone off at the knees is something painful, bloody and I'm assuming, in some states, illegal.

IS IT EVER TOO LATE TO HAVE STANDARDS?

Dear Greg and Amiira,

How do I tell a guy that I've been going out with for two months that I'm not okay with some of the things I pretended to be okay with when we first started dating? I really like him and he fits into my idea of what I want in a man (good job, doesn't do drugs, owns his own home and is really good looking) so I let some things slide that I thought weren't that big of a deal to me. It seemed like a good trade-off for what he did have at the time, but now it's not working for me. After our first date he suggested that it'd be easier for us to meet at restaurants instead of him picking me up since I live on the other side of town. I agreed because it seemed logical, but now it makes me feel like I'm not worth driving fifteen minutes for. He told me that he doesn't like having me sleep over because he sleeps better in the bed alone and needs a good night's sleep in order to do his job well. So when we go back to his place and get intimate I always feel like he's watching the clock and waiting for me to leave. It sounds bad, but the relationship is going well and I know he's not seeing anyone else but rather just set in his ways. Do you think these are deal breakers and how do I renegotiate the terms of our dating life?

Arabelle

Paris, France

Dear Bait and Switcher,

You've got to come clean, kiddo. You set the bar low and now you are living at it. As you pointed out, it's not his fault. This is what he thinks is standard operating procedure for you and it works for him. It's what guys refer to as the old Bait and Switch. You've sold him this version of you that doesn't require some of the basics of dating. Now you are going to have to set him straight and tell him that you've changed your mind, then understand if he buckles at the idea of doing things differently. As for things that don't work for him like sleeping over, why are you letting him decide what's okay for you? Relationships are a negotiation where both parties get to have their needs met and accommodated. BOTH—as in you, too. In the future, be clear about what you want from the beginning and you can't go wrong.

IS RELIGION A STANDARD OR A DEAL BREAKER?

Dear Greg and Amiira,

I'm 29 years old, Jewish and single. My family is not conveniently Jewish as in we like an extra day off work, we are actively Jewish to the point that my mother is insistent that I marry a Jewish man or I will break her heart and the Torah will burst into the flames or something else that's really bad. I'm not saying that I won't marry a Jewish guy, but I am keeping my options open to finding the best man for me, then dealing with religion later. Does religion fall under deal breakers or standards, and what defines the difference in this particular case?

Eliza
Beverly Hills, CA

Dear Torah Destroyah,

Faith usually helps sets a standard by which we decide to live our lives. *Greg's experience with it is this:* I was not brought up in a spiritual home. When I was thirty-three I got sober and turned my life over to a "power greater than myself" and I live my life by a set of spiritual principals. For the longest time I would only date sober girls, figuring that they would be the only ones who would understand me. Well, that turned out not to be the case. Those actually turned out to be some of the most volatile relationships I'd ever been in. So I finally opened the door to dating others and lo and behold I met someone more spiritually compatible than anyone I had met in my program. So I chose to pick the person who made me feel the most spiritually sound rather than of my particular faith.

Amiira's experience with it is this: My father is a very Catholic man. He goes to church every Sunday, come hell or high water, and practices his faith daily. My mother was not Catholic and did not like the Catholic Church's position on women in general forty-plus years ago when they met. My mother was not willing to convert, and my father wanted to be with her more than he wanted to be with someone who was Catholic but wasn't her. They married and had children (me being one of them). My mother did not want her children brought up in the Catholic Church so we weren't. That being said, my father practices his religion fully supported by his wife and children. I love how important my father's religion is to him and I love that my mother makes sure that his schedule is clear on Sundays so that he can make it to church. Their relationship is strengthened by their respect for their differences. Religion can be a great divider or the glue in a most unexpected way.

None of these examples might enlighten your plight, but here's a thought: the narrower we make the door, the fewer get in.

WHAT IF A DEAL BREAKER IS UNFAIR?

Dear Greg and Amiira,

Matthew and I have been going out for seven months, and I thought things were not only going well but that we were definitely headed for the altar. We are like two peas in a pod. We get along great, have the same sense of humor, and the sex is the best I've ever had. So you can imagine how completely surprised I was when he broke up with me and cited the fact that I am taller than him as the reason that he doesn't want to get serious with me. What is that all about? How can my height be a big enough deal that he's ending a great relationship? It's not like I was short when we met and started dating then grew. I've been 5'11" since the first time he asked if he could buy me a drink, and I was even wearing heels that night. Matthew says he can't marry a woman who's taller than he is and that even though he loves me it's a deal breaker for him. What can I do?

Delphine
Madison, WI

Dear Delphine the Devastated,

Sadly, there are people in this world that let great relationships go because of some preconceived and narrow-minded idea about what the right person for them must look or be like. Though it sucks to be on the other end of it, sounds like you got out at just the right time. Who wants to spend eternity with someone who willfully won't love you because of your height? Or maybe he feels small around you and can't get past it. We can't always help how someone makes us feel about ourselves. Either way it would have spelled out a miserable future together, even if your past was a great one. The best things in life come in completely different packages than we expect them to, but some people resist that idea all the way to the grave. Just remember that some of the most beautiful women in the world are tall ones. Anyone ever heard of models?

FROM THE OTHER SIDE OF THE FENCE

WHEN SHOULD I SETTLE?

Dear Greg and Amiira,

I believe there are girls you have fun with and girls you bring home to meet the folks, you know what I mean? As an equal opportunity dater I've been able to fine-tune my ideas of the perfect woman, and when I find her I'll marry her. The perfect woman has her own job, life and income. The perfect woman can tell a joke, take a joke, play one-on-one hoop and know the difference between every major sport. She must love sex and be good at it but not have had it with more than two people a year after the age of 18. She's stronger than she looks (emotionally and physically), smarter than she is beautiful, and loyal to her friends and family above all. My friends and I call this the Quest For The Perfect Ten, but I've been coming up empty-handed for a few years now. I've asked my sisters what points they think I should settle on, but they just rolled their eyes and dared me to ask you. So do I settle or hold out?

Lucas
Wichita, KS

Dear Dumbass,

You forgot about the kind of girls you let wash your pickup truck. I'm sure you're probably a perfect ten yourself ... except for being a little short on intelligence and endowment. Good luck with that.

THE CHICK THAT BLEW IT

So I had been kind of fooling around with this girl that I thought was amazing. She was beautiful, sexy, cool and really smart. We had so much in common and our chemistry was palpable. For months I tried to get her to promote me to being her boyfriend and take me and us seriously. She would always just tell me she couldn't entertain the idea of something serious now, she didn't have the capacity to devote the time and effort because she was so busy with work. I did everything right. I treated her like a queen, always did little things to let her know I was thinking about her and was nothing but available and interested. Then one night after a few too many of the drinkie-poos as she liked to call them (the only uncool thing about her) she finally fessed up that she could never really respect a guy that didn't make more money than she did and that's why she wouldn't be my girlfriend. That admission was like a punch to the solar plexus. Here I was in love with this girl, and she didn't respect me because of money? At the time I was launching an Internet marketing company out of my studio apartment that she thought was an excuse not to have a "real job." So that was that and it was almost five years ago. Well cut to last week and I see her at an event that my company's promoting, and she makes her way over to ask how I've been. It was like the best moment of my life when I got to look her in the eye and tell her, "Things are great. I just sold my company for 20 million. How are you?" I'm telling you she went ashen. Then the next three weeks she left me seven voicemails and sent about thirty texts, all of which went unanswered.

Jonah

Laguna Beach, CA

MAYBE YOU GUYS ARE RIGHT

Most of my relationships since college have been wildly unsuccessful, and I think of myself as a relatively easygoing person. I've always been able to overlook a flaw or forty when it comes to guys if they're good people. Then I finally realized that guys with forty or more flaws are actually not that great of a catch. So I decided that I needed to take a look at my standards and give them some updating. I figured out that my problem wasn't that my standards were low; it was just that I wasn't sticking to them or, worse yet, I was letting other things override them or make up for things that were lacking. Like if I was dating a guy who had never been able to be monogamous but was really convincing when he said he thought he might be able to stay faithful to me, then I'd make an exception on my "Won't date cheaters" standard. How do you think that one paid off for me? That was nine months ago that I recognized

.. error of my ways and decided that I was sticking to my guns with a new "No Bending" rule to my standards. I'm not going to lie that it's been slim pickings because most guys don't live their lives or make choices that rise to my level of standards; HOWEVER, the few guys that I have met who do are much better guys than I have ever dated before. It's a total quality over quantity reversal. Though I'm not currently in a relationship, I know that when I am it will be a good one because I will have finally chosen someone capable of having a good relationship because he too will live a life of standards.

Marissa

Edinburgh, Scotland

FIRST PERSON SINGLE, BY AMIIRA

Compromising my standards used to be a full-time job for me. I'd do it for work, I'd do it for friends, I'd do it to fit in, and I'd certainly do it for love, almost love, and even like. Looking back at myself, it's so clear the things I could not see (or didn't want to see) in the men I chose. Their blatant limitations, unfixable flaws in character or outright trespasses and my *choice* to not see them. I'm not blind or dumb about men … I'm worse. I'm a deliberate overlooker. I will forgive you many sins if you make me laugh. A great sense of humor will get you everywhere with me and I'm not proud of it. But don't think I didn't suffer for being such a pushover because I was put through the ringer by some of these underdeveloped but funny boys. I was convinced that I could fill in the blanks for these guys or fix them or help them grow up or whatever it was that I had assessed them with a deficiency of. You know what I learned over and over again with every disappointment? You can't fix people or make them change; the only thing you can do is pack your shit and leave if it isn't working for you. Though I tested that "can't change people" theory over and over again I found it to be true. So instead of trying to fix or change others I concentrated on what was going on with me. What I discovered was that my self-esteem had taken a few beatings, that I looked for validatic from broken men, and that funny isn't enough on its own— it takes substance as well. I revisited all my past relationships and thought about those men, their limitations and flaws as well as my own and I made a mental checklist of places I wouldn't be going again. Emotionally unavailable or stunted would no longer be seeing my face. Compulsive liar and cowardly actions were off my Christmas card list. Can't get his shit together or dig his way out of a hole with a shovel and a map were plummeting down the charts. Wildly selfish and has no concern for others was tied to an anchor and sinking. But you know what made a big comeback? My own value, the things I truly see value in and a higher standard by which I choose to live and fill my life. That's when my life started to go from being good to great. We have complete control over the most important thing that will determine your path in life and that is the standards by which *you* decide to live.

THOUGHTS FROM MAN CITY

I have to admit I know a thing or two about standards. Probably because I really didn't used to have any. Well let's be fair; I knew what tequila went best with tequila, and that at nighttime it's best to sleep indoors—whose bed didn't really matter. Let me tell you this: a life without standards can end pretty badly, so when I was thirty-three I made the decision to get drinks free. (Remember?) That doesn't make me special; it's just the right choice for me. At one of the meetings that I attended in an effort to stay sober, someone said the phrase "Stick with the winners." Meaning, I guess, hang with those who have what you want in life, the ones that live up to an ideal and principles you can identify with. That afternoon I was wandering around a mall looking at stuff I couldn't afford to buy when I met a winner. A toaster. "Drunk again?" you ask. No, quite the opposite, actually. Some people refer to it as a moment of clarity. I was looking at the window display of the Williams Sonoma when I saw, in all its polished glory, the Dualit four-slice, stainless steel toaster. The one with the two wide slots that, according to the salesperson, makes the natural leap from toast to toasted sandwiches. For some reason this household appliance with all of its toasting dexterity struck me as EXTRAORDINARY. I know that sounds insane and maybe it was, but I was newly "drinks free" and I was hanging on by a very thin thread. It seemed to be the most evolved and full-blown version of a toaster that could be. It had in its very design a sense of pride and dignity. This toaster wasn't just content to make toast; it was about a toaster lifestyle. By virtue of its aesthetic this toaster was challenging everything around it to the same standard of excellence that it was living at. I felt the toaster was asking me to answer questions like: "Who is the man that owns this toaster and what's his life like? Who is the girl that dates the man that owns this toaster, and what kind of life do they have when they are standing around the toaster eating toast and/or toasted sandwiches?" I felt that this toaster was advocating a better life. I mean, after all, isn't that what great design is supposed to do? It was so inspiring in fact that for days it was all I could obsess about instead of wanting a drink. It moved me to write, which I had not, with the exception of my phone number on some cocktail napkins, ever done. I also got a job because I wanted to buy this toaster and also pay rent, which seemed of primary importance to my roommate. Roommates can be sticky like that. Over time I wrote a one-man show about it called "Mantastic" that eventually became an HBO special. It's the same special that convinced my wife to go on a date with me. (I sent her an advanced copy, which I strongly suggest you do as well if you have one.) Now the Dualit, four-slice, stainless steel toaster with the two wide slots that make the natural leap from toast to toasted sandwiches sits with great pride in my kitchen today making toast for my girls every morning. But more than that, it reminds me every day of who I am and who I want to be and the level my life needs to be lived at. It is the standard by which I live my life because I'm the guy that owns it. Toast?

DATING FORTUNE COOKIE

Live well and the world will open its doors. Live poorly and the world will slam them in your face and go back to playing cards with its buddies.

WORST DATE EVER

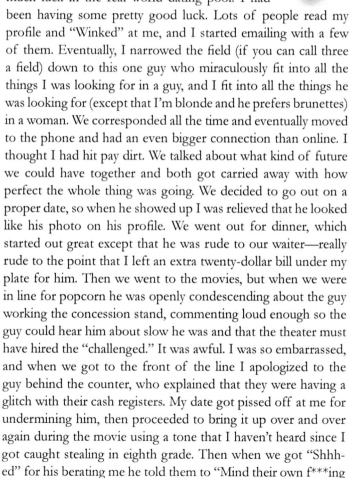

I had been trying online dating since I hadn't had much luck in the real world dating pool. I had been having some pretty good luck. Lots of people read my profile and "Winked" at me, and I started emailing with a few of them. Eventually, I narrowed the field (if you can call three a field) down to this one guy who miraculously fit into all the things I was looking for in a guy, and I fit into all the things he was looking for (except that I'm blonde and he prefers brunettes) in a woman. We corresponded all the time and eventually moved to the phone and had an even bigger connection than online. I thought I had hit pay dirt. We talked about what kind of future we could have together and both got carried away with how perfect the whole thing was going. We decided to go out on a proper date, so when he showed up I was relieved that he looked like his photo on his profile. We went out for dinner, which started out great except that he was rude to our waiter—really rude to the point that I left an extra twenty-dollar bill under my plate for him. Then we went to the movies, but when we were in line for popcorn he was openly condescending about the guy working the concession stand, commenting loud enough so the guy could hear him about slow he was and that the theater must have hired the "challenged." It was awful. I was so embarrassed, and when we got to the front of the line I apologized to the guy behind the counter, who explained that they were having a glitch with their cash registers. My date got pissed off at me for undermining him, then proceeded to bring it up over and over again during the movie using a tone that I haven't heard since I got caught stealing in eighth grade. Then when we got "Shhh-ed" for his berating me he told them to "Mind their own f***ing business," followed by a generalized sexual preference slur. It was mortifying. Here's this guy who I thought was everything I wanted in a guy—had my whole checklist covered, *something that has never happened for me before*, and he was the worst guy I've ever met and shitty to every person that crossed his path. I hadn't even thought to put "Not A Shitty Person" on the list because I assumed that would be a given, but apparently not. Needless to say, our date ended abruptly after that because I walked out of the theater in the dark and blocked him from my online profile and my mobile phone. As it turns out, my standards of what's right for human behavior is much are more important than my deal breakers or wish lists.

IT'S JUST A F***ING STANDARD

You know what you want. You always have. And if you don't remember, let us tell you. You want to be happy and you want to be in a relationship where you can feel comfortable with who you are because you picked someone who honors the very essence of you. Finding happiness is going to be harder for you if it's based on height requirement. So set standards that are attainable for people striving for greatness regardless of hair color or yearly income. Trust us, your whole life goes better when you live by a set of standards, because they teach people how to treat you.

THE ORIGINAL WORLD FAMOUS WINNER DATER'S WORKBOOK

Now that you've read about the differences between Standards and Deal Breakers let's see if you can spot which is which. Check the box for Standard or Deal Breaker.

1. Must have tight red curly hair

2. Believes in God

3. Has traveled outside the country he was born in

4. Must believe in Bon Jovi

5. Doesn't eat red meat

6. Can speak more than one language

7. Owns his own home

8. Likes Indian food

9. Is under forty-five years of age

10. Has a full head of hair

11. Likes my kids

12. Calls when he says he's going to

13. Doesn't do drugs

14. Has ambition

15. Can't have any female friends

Turn the page to see the answers.

1, 3, 4, 5, 6, 7, 8, 9, 10, 15 are all Deal Breakers

2, 11, 12, 13, 14 are all Standards

PRINCIPLE #7
DON'T SHOW THE MOVIE
BEFORE THE TRAILER!

Anticipation, Seduction and the
Fine Art of Waiting to Have Sex

Here's a great way to think about sex and dating. Think of yourself as a summer blockbuster movie, or more specifically that having sex with you is a summer blockbuster movie. Now, with such a highly anticipated event you don't just open it without any fanfare, right? What about a teaser? How about the trailer? Think about it. Don't Show the Movie Before the Trailer is a philosophy and a strategy all rolled into one. Close your eyes. Now imagine it's Christmastime and you're in the movie theatre to see some holiday triumph-of-the-human-spirit flick. You're settled into your seat with your popcorn, Junior Mints and Diet Pepsi … then the lights go dark, the curtains open, then BOOM! A giant glowing version of the Iron Man logo slams against the screen. It vanishes as quickly as it arrived and then you see the numbers: 7-4-14. The whole thing lasts less than ten seconds but it's thrilling. It's the teaser, and it's a wildly effective way of letting people know that something great is coming. Anticipation is the greatest aphrodisiac in the world, so if you like him and want him to stick around then don't show him the whole movie right away. Let him check out the teaser early on, like a long hot kiss and the mention of things to come. The teaser gives him the complete understanding that yes, you'd like to show him the feature but it's still a ways away from the opening. (Again, pun intended.)

Then comes the trailer—two- to three-minute preview of the most exciting, emotional and sexy parts of the movie cut together to tell you enough of the story as they can without revealing the ending in the hope that you won't be able to contain yourself until it opens. Making out in your underwear is a great trailer. The point of the teaser and the trailer is to make the actual movie (the first time you have sex) matter. No one is suggesting that you remain chaste until your wedding night, but what we are saying is there is real value to building up to the actual event instead of just doing it. When you have sex quickly you're overlooking the glory of foreplay and anticipation, which are some of the premiere parts of the sexual experience. You only get this part, the newness, the beginning of the relationship ONCE—*you can't get it again*. Why would you want to rush through it when you could draw it out and really savor it for all its deliciousness. There is only ONE *first kiss*, ONE *first touch*, ONE *first time you have sex* together; why not make each one memorable? Anticipation = memorable. Seriously. If you didn't have to think of it before it happened, you most likely won't remember it that much after it happened. We don't know if you've heard the news, but going the speed of light only serves the space program.

Sex is where people get the most screwed (pun intended) in dating. If you have sex **too soon** with someone you really like, you have a pretty good shot of f***ing up the relationship. The problem is when people want to get into a serious relationship, they have sex too casually, hoping it will expedite the process and create intimacy, when in fact it often has the opposite effect. Sex is an intimate act, and you cannot underestimate the power it has on two people when they hardly know one another. Sex changes things, even if you don't want it to or continue to pretend that it doesn't. People feel differently about each other after they've done it. Sometimes they feel closer, sometimes they feel weirder, sometimes they feel confused and sometimes they feel the beginning of the end. That's why we suggest that you can't lose by waiting to have sex until you get to know someone better, but you can totally blow it by having sex too fast. We've spoken to every guy we know and they all agree that having sex changes how they feel about a woman. (Wow, what a revelation!) But here's the interesting thing: many of the guys we talked to said that a lot of times, when they have sex with a girl they don't know very well, that as soon as it's done, they're over her, and they don't know why it is, because she's still all the things she was before they did it. People don't always know why there's an internal shift, and it's not always intentional, but sex triggers the "get me out of here" button in many men (and women, for that matter), but it happens less to those that go slower.

We are not now, nor have we ever been, against casual sex. In fact, we think that's all you should have from college until your mid-forties. Okay, that's not true. We think if you are comfortable with having casual sex then rock the sheets, and if used properly casual sex can be a great learning tool as you evolve into a person who eventually wants to get into serious relationships (and has some good moves in the sack). We are talking about two different things here, so let's be clear. There's the "I really like this guy and I want to have sex with him." And the "I'm just looking for someone to have a naked party with." If you're falling into the earlier category, you have to decide when is the right time for you to have sex. Is it before you know each other? (PROBABLY NOT/RESOUNDING NO!) Is it after you know each other a little better? (MAYBE, BUT ACTUALLY NO.) OR is it after you're both emotionally invested enough that it won't freak one of you out or make it a relationship based on sex? (HELLS YEAH!) We like the idea of setting up a mental checklist of things that you only know about a person after you've spent some quality time with them. Once you know the details of the things on your list and many other juicy nuggets of information, not only will you have a better knowledge or your future sex mate but probably a deeper fondness. And that will make the sex even more rocking!

Example:
How they take their coffee.

Which commercials make them angry and which ones make them nostalgic.

What they call their grandma and what Grandma calls them.

A detailed account of their high school formal dance.

Their most embarrassing moment.

What they really like to do on Sundays when they're not trying to impress you.

What they can tell you about you. (Do they know what you do for a living? Can they spell your last name?)

What they are like after ten dates. (Gotcha on that one.)

Look, guys can find a girl to just have casual sex with, but you get to decide if you're that girl. If you really like someone and want to have a shot at having a great relationship with them ... DON'T BE THAT GIRL.

BUT GREG AND AMIIRA, I HAVE QUESTIONS!

BUT WHAT IF I WAITED AND HE STILL BAILED?

Dear Greg and Amiira,

Okay, I saw you both on The Today Show and you said something about waiting to have sex with a guy if you really like him. Well I took your idea to heart. At the time I was falling pretty hard for this musician named Pete who was ridiculously hot. I'm no dummy and I wasn't going to sleep with him right away just because he was in a band, but then I heard you guys and decided to really make him work for it. We waited almost two months! He was on and off the road, to be fair, so it's not like it was completely because of my will. Well, finally we did it and it was awesome. I was so glad we waited I hadn't ever done that. But guess what? Three days after the big night he broke it off? What gives? I WAITED and he still bailed right after we had sex.

Nova

New York City

P.S. His band totally sucked.

Dear Band Aid,

Obviously there are no guarantees in life and people, especially musicians, can be weird; it's just a fact. (Look it up on Wikipedia if you won't take my word for it.) That said, aren't you glad you gave it your best shot? Would it have been better if you had slept with him on the third date and then never heard from him, always wondering what you could have done better? You respected yourself and the situation, and for that you should feel great. You tried to get to know someone before getting intimate with him—that's just smart living. We know that doesn't take the pain away, but some guys are only going to be in it for the sex—it just happens. But that doesn't mean that you aren't a great person. In the long run you have succeeded in becoming a person who runs their life differently, and we suspect you will attract an even better man next time, or at least one from a better band.

BUT WHAT IF WE WON'T SEE EACH OTHER AGAIN FOR TWO MONTHS?

Dear Greg and Amiira,

I met this terrific gentleman online. The problem is, and always seems to be, that we live in different towns. He lives in Libertyville, Illinois and I live in San Carlos, California. We were online for a month and then we switched to the phone, texting, and instant messaging. We communicate all day every day. We've seen multiple pictures of one another (all clothed Ha Ha!) and we seem to be really attracted to each other. Here's my question. Obviously our texts and e-mails have gotten flirty and a little sexual. Now he's coming to visit me for the weekend. He's getting a hotel, but I feel like we are going to both want to have sex even though this is the first time we've been in person together. Is that the wrong move? I don't want to lose this guy, but is this too early? What if we can't see each other for another couple of months?

Bethany
San Carlos, CA

Dear Cyberdater,

No, we don't think you should have sex with him, and here's why ... It's your FIRST REAL DATE. Chances are the moment he steps off the plane it's going to become really real for both of you and possibly a bit awkward because that's when he becomes a person. In fact, we bet you don't start feeling comfortable with one another until half way through the trip, and only then will you know if this is a person worth being with at all. Sex changes things. It just does, and right now you are on a winning streak. So keep it in check until the next time. If there is real heat between you, we bet you don't wait two months to see each other.

BUT WHAT IF SEX IS THE ONLY WAY TO KEEP HIM?

Dear Greg and Amiira,

I really liked this guy Liam, and we dated for about a month before it became clear that we were at a standoff. I really didn't want to sleep with him until he had stopped sleeping with other women, and he wasn't ready to commit to being only with me. So things got tense between us, and it seemed like it was all going to be ruined if I didn't give in. So I slept with him, figuring that he would be so happy that I had given in and like me even more, then stop seeing the other women. Well that didn't happen, and now I'm just one of three women he's seeing, and I don't even know if I'm at the top of the three or the bottom. What do I do now that he's having his cake and eating it too?

Birdie
London, England

Dear London Bridges,

How come your London Bridges are always falling down? We don't need to tell you that you shouldn't have caved in for this guy; you already learned that painful lesson. What we will tell you is that in the future if you want to be in a monogamous relationship then don't have sex until you have defined the relationship as such—NO EXCEPTIONS. As for the having and eating his cake, the only thing you can do is take it away from him and save it for someone who will truly appreciate you and not make you wonder if you're bringing home the gold, silver or bronze medal in the lady Olympics.

HOW DO YOU TURN CASUAL SEX INTO ACTUAL DATING?

Dear Amiira and Greg,

*My lab partner and I started hooking up during our lab sessions and now I'm screwed. We see each other all the time between class, lab sessions and extra curricular hooking up, but every time I try to get him to ask me out on a proper date he shuts me down. He says dating is too much pressure and that he's not really into "Old School" dating. We go to a very prestigious school, so you'd think he'd be able to handle pressure a little better. What the f***?! How do I convert this thing from being a casual sex thing into more of a dating exclusively thing?*

Maggie

Vancouver, Canada

Dear Lab-orious,

Wake up, Maggie; we think we've got something to say to you. You set the tone for this thing from the beginning and attracted the kind of guy who, according to you, can't handle the "pressure" of dating you. Let's see how he handles the pressure of not getting to have sex with you as you back off this ridiculous relationship you set up for yourself. If dating is what you want then dating is what you do and NOTHING ELSE. Tell Grabby the lab partner that you've tested the theory and run the data but his lack of effort less than equals the glory of getting down with you. If the thought of getting to continue having sex with you at some point isn't motivation enough for him to ask you out then you have your answer (He's Just Not That Into You), and if you need backup we'll send you the book.

FROM THE OTHER SIDE OF THE FENCE

WHAT DOES WAITING TO HAVE SEX REALLY MEAN?

Dear Greg and Amiira,

Okay, so I'm a bloke and I've read your books, so clearly I'm messed up. I've been seeing this bird for two months now. We have the best time hanging out, skateboarding and going to shows. But she will not have sex with me. I feel like she likes me because we snog (she's a good kisser) and whatever (meaning things that could be considered foreplay), but she says she wants to wait to have sex. She's not a Christian or anything; in fact, I know she's slept with some other guys that she dated before sooner. Maybe I misunderstood your book, but is she not into me?

Blake

Bristol, England

Dear Sensitive Skatepunk,

We think you did misunderstand what we said in *He's Just Not That Into You.* In that book we said if someone isn't interested in being sexual with you then you might want to consider that they are not that into you. She is in fact being sexual with you; maybe she hasn't slept with you because she really likes you and sleeping with guys too quickly in the past hasn't worked for her. If it's not working for you then break it off, but if you're still getting hot kisses and whatnot, what's the hurry? You still ride a skateboard and go to concerts, so you're young at heart at the minimum. Enjoy the anticipation of what might be to come; it'll be a far better ride than the wipeout you'll have if you pressure her into having sex out of obligation rather than pure desire.

THE CHICK WHO BLEW IT

It's hard to say "No" to a girl who wants to have sex with you on the first date. It's always pretty fun, but afterwards it's so weird. What does she think it means? Does she think that we're going out now? Should I sleep over or go? Will she be mad if I go? The sex on the first date is tough because obviously I liked her enough to ask her out but, and I know it's a terrible thing to say, once you have sex the game of cat and mouse is over. You've already gotten the cheese. So I had been really jocking this girl Chloe to go out with me, and she was playing hard to get/couldn't care less for the longest time. Then I finally broke her down and she agreed to having lunch with me during the week. Is lunch on a Wednesday even a date? So I went to her house to pick her up and she wasn't dressed yet. She walked from her bedroom to her bathroom in her bra and underwear right in front of me and I was thinking, "Oh, man please put on some clothes because I really like you and we need to go out to lunch or I'm screwed." Well she didn't get dressed; in fact, she just threw on an open robe and came and sat on the couch and suggested we watch TV. TV turned into making out, which turned into having sex. I kept thinking, I can be different, this time will be different, but the truth is that I tend to lose interest with women that sleep with me on the first date. It's such a terrible thing to say, but I couldn't go out with someone who gives it up so easily, because if they're giving it up for me, how many others have gotten in on the action too? I can't believe I'm admitting that to you. I sound like a shit. Sex is different than love, and even though we love having sex we'd trade good, easy sex in for a great love any day of the week.

Scott

Scottsdale, AZ

MAYBE YOU GUYS ARE RIGHT

Every relationship I've ever had started sexually before emotionally. I'm twenty-eight now and have never had a relationship that lasted longer than three months because somehow the sexual relationship didn't translate into an emotional one on both sides. More accurately, the guys never got as invested as I did and things just kind of fizzled out. Then when I met Josh, I decided to take your advice and wait to have sex with him. I thought that waiting four dates would seem like an eternity, but when we got to date four I realized that I really liked how things were going and I wasn't ready to change the dynamic of it yet by having sex, so I decided to wait until the sixth date. Then date six rolls around and he mentions something like, "… when you meet my parents you'll see what I mean." We had yet to have sex and he could see me meeting his parents in the future! Unheard of. So date six blows by and on date eight, when things are already going better than with any other guy I've ever dated, he says that he'd like it if I were his girlfriend. You have no idea what that felt like for me. If I could have stopped time I would have so I could leap right out of my seat and do a happy dance. So eight was the magic number, and that night we had sex and it was the greatest first sex I've ever had in my life. If I had known how much better sex is when you have significant feelings (other than lust) for someone, I would have waited way before now. I guess I thought that sex was the way to get a guy, but what I learned is that it's not the way to keep one. Guys stay when they like more than just having sex with you.

Vivianne
New Haven, CT

FIRST PERSON SINGLE, BY AMIIRA

Not that I should be applauded for my sex life, but aside from one exception, I've always been one to keep my pants on. Not that I'm a prude or don't enjoy sex, but strong is my desire to keep the membership to my super secret private club lower than the number of digits in my phone number (including area code … and international calling code. Wait, how many is that?) Keeping my number low was a source of self-respect and not surprisingly a crazy turn on for the Don Juans applying for a membership. When I started dating someone new, it wasn't until we really knew each other and were dating exclusively that I showed them the secret handshake and laminated their membership card. Then one time I threw out the winning recipe and slept with a guy that I really liked on the second date. I thought what the hell, why not? We're on the right track, he likes me, I like him, what difference can it make? So we had sex, then went out for breakfast the next morning, me thinking, "Wow, this is nice. I guess waiting isn't all that necessary." Clearly, I was thinking that he and I were on the same page, that I was a good judge of character, and that we were probably pretty much going out after having slept together. He, on the other hand, wasn't even in the same book much less on the same page as me, as he saw fit to take home an "exotic dancer" the next night that needed a ride, and didn't resurface for three days. Not only did it hurt my feelings that he slept with someone else, but I was totally embarrassed for being so wrong about what

I thought it had been and what we were moving towards. It only took once for me to learn the lesson that sex upfront doesn't always pay in the end; not only that but the sex wasn't good enough to outweigh how shitty it made me feel. Now, you may not think that all guys will be okay with waiting, but let me tell you a story. I used to work in the music business so I worked with fledgling bands and rock stars, all of whom are used to having ladies give up the goods shortly after the initial "Hey, great show." A good majority of those same (aspiring and established) rock gods delighted at the idea of nailing one of the chicks from the record company, so even when I was married to my first husband I was propositioned quite often. While it was flattering and a little lame at the same time, I learned to deflect their advances and keep my job. A flirty little "I don't think I can expense condoms and a hotel room but thanks for thinking of me" always did the trick and interestingly enough, every time my rejected rockers came into town it was my office that they would park their asses in to try to make headway into my super secret private club. During these headway sessions, what happened is that we got to know each other, and so I was the one they would call from the road for advice about how to get rid of some other record company girl they had gotten busy with, then pledge their love to me and tell me how it would be different if I finally gave in (which I didn't, by the way). The thing that became clear to me was that even the most happening guy wants to be told "NO" and not only that, is titillated to try to work harder for it. Seems to me that having sex early can be a rocking good time but isn't always the shortcut to a good relationship. More often than not it's the road away from one.

THOUGHTS FROM MAN CITY

You ladies run the show. I know many of you don't think you do, but YOU DO! With the exception of some extreme assholes, we guys will pretty much do only what you let us. Example: If you let us come over at 4:00 a.m. for a "snack" then we're coming over, BUT if you say we have to wait a few weeks until we know each other better then WE WILL WAIT. If we can't wait … well then we only *ever* wanted to just have sex with you in the first place. Sorry, ladies, but it's the truth. I know you think you have to have sex with us or we're going to leave, but if sex is all we want WE'RE GOING TO LEAVE ANYWAY. That's how I see it. I'm just me. Whenever I had sex with a woman too early on, here's what would happen: My head would be so clouded with the idea of having sex that I often wasn't sure whether I liked them or just wanted to "do it" because sex is on guys' minds much of the time. Then as soon as I would orgasm I'd realize "Oh, I only wanted sex" OR "Wow, I don't even know this person!" It would be awkward and often I'd bail. Now I take full responsibility for my actions. It wasn't the girl's fault we had sex too early or that I wasn't emotionally able to handle it, but I think this is a common problem for many men. We are not sure which end of it we're on in the early stages—if it's sex or a relationship that we want. Since I believe that women are the gatekeepers to sex, I'd have to tell you that if you want to be sure a guy's there for more than sex—KEEP THE GATES LOCKED FOR A BIT. You might be interested to know that many of us want you to make us work for it. That there is great pleasure in not getting what you want right off the bat. It makes you work harder to get it. And along the way we get to know you better, know your taste in music, wine, clothes, how many cats you have, your brother's name, and why we like you in the first place besides your smile and sweet-smelling skin. So if you like us and are interested in more than just sex, make it a challenge. Any guy who calls you a tease is a CHUMP. It's not a tease; it is, as we discussed earlier in this chapter, a preview to a movie that we are so glad we got cast in.

DATING FORTUNE COOKIE

Sex is the way to reach an orgasm, not a commitment.

WORST DATE EVER

I liked this guy forever and thought he would never ask me out because I saw him all the time, but he never even looked in my general direction. Then one night he walked over to me and my friends at the bar we all hang out at and told me with a smile that it really hurt his feelings that I hadn't asked him out yet. I laughed at his little pick up line, and we spent the rest of the night talking, drinking and flirting. Then he asked if he could come home with me, and I know I shouldn't have let him but I did. So we went back to my place and had mind-blowing sex. We were up all night talking, having sex and then snacking naked at the fridge. It was one of my best nights ever. I had liked this guy from afar for so long and he was as great as I hoped he would be. So before going our separate ways in the morning we decided to meet back at the bar around eight o'clock that night. I went to work and called every last one of my girlfriends and told them about my scandalous yet awesome night and invited them all to come meet us for drinks. So I get to the bar with my girlfriends and I'm waiting for him to show and it's eight o'clock, then eight thirty, then nine o'clock, then nine thirty and there's no sign of him. At ten fifteen he comes rolling in with another girl! So I go up to him and tell him that I've been waiting for him since eight at night, and he plays completely dumb like he has no idea what I'm talking about. So I say, "Are you going to introduce me to your friend?" Now I'm totally feeling like a crazy jealous woman trying not to lose my shit. And he says, "I would if I knew your name." Then he and his girl breezed past me like I was a nut job and sat in another room in a booth with his back turned to where I was so he wouldn't have to see me. I've never been so embarrassed and humiliated in my whole life.

IT'S JUST F***ING SEX

Don't get us wrong, sex *is* one of the more awesome aspects of being human. That's why it should be respected as such when it comes to love. Sex doesn't solve problems or solidify relationships. What we believe sex should be is an enhancement to what should already exist, like friendship, trust and a mutual respect for the artistry of Arcade Fire. Give sex its due, put it in its proper place and it will serve you better.

THE ORIGINAL WORLD FAMOUS WINNER DATER'S WORKBOOK

It's time to make your checklist of things you should know about the guy (or gal) you're thinking about having sex with. The list must be comprised of things that you couldn't possibly know about him without having invested many dates' and hours' worth of conversation to uncover. While you're at it, why don't you make a list of things he should know about you before he gets to know what you look like in the buff. We'll start you off with a few, then you're on!

What I Want to Know About Him

1. What's one thing he's always wanted to try (*that's not related to sex*)?

2. Where did his parents meet?

3. Favorite band, favorite record, favorite song, favorite movie

4.

5.

6.

7.

8.

9.

10.

What I Want Him to Know About Me

1. What my favorite thing is on the menu at three different restaurants

2. Who your best friend is and what she looks like *(that means he's got to meet your friends)*

3. Favorite smell

4.

5.

6.

7.

8.

9.

10.

PRINCIPLE #8
NOT EVERY DATE IS GOING TO TURN INTO A RELATIONSHIP

And a Worthwhile Relationship Is a Marathon, Not a Sprint

There's nothing quite like the feeling of meeting someone new. Your whole body is awake and alive, your mind is buzzing—it's as if your entire being is vibrating at another frequency. The speed at which thoughts and ideas occur as you see flashes of your future is dizzying and thrilling. It's the exhilaration of new like and possibly future love.

There you are in line for a coffee when he asks for the time. You oblige with the information and blush when he admits to already having a watch and just using the time as an excuse to talk to you. Two hours later, you're still at the coffee shop talking animatedly and kind of falling for this cute guy with an English pop star haircut that's asking you to dinner. He kisses you on the cheek after entering your digits into his mobile phone and cementing dinner plans for the next night. All the way home you nearly levitate with the giddiness of liking someone new that you "totally connect with" for the first time in a long time. For the next thirty-six hours until your dinner date with the cute guy from the coffee shop (or at least the ones that you're conscious for), you think about him, replay the kiss goodbye, think about what to wear, tell your friends about him, remember what his smile looked like, wonder where he grew up and whether his parents still live there, wonder if you'll like his parents, think about how cute you'll look together walking around the city on the weekends, wonder if he'll move into your place or you'll move into his, feel the relief of having a date for your sister's wedding, wonder if the wedding will get him thinking about marriage, debate keeping your own name or taking his when the two of you get married, replay the kiss goodbye, think about what you're going to wear to dinner, wonder if you'll get married in a church or outdoors, envision the two of you running amidst the pouring grains of rice to climb into the car with "Just Married" written in soap on the rearview window, replay the moment he admitted that the time was just an excuse to talk to you, and on and it goes until dinner with the dreamboat. The future looks bright … then he never calls and your *end resulting** only results in being more crushed than necessary. (* *End resulting being when you play a scenario so far out in the future in your head that you become invested in the future or end result instead of the present reality.*)

There's something intoxicating about liking someone new and thinking that "this might be it." We can't help ourselves; we just race into the future with our thoughts and desires because we want that thing that we don't have. We want to lock down our future happiness so we know that we're not going to miss out. It's the place where desire and desperation meet. It doesn't feel desperate because the rush of feelings is so yummy, but the "end resulting" is a manifestation of fear that we might miss out. That's not to say that you shouldn't get the future that you want, just that you're less likely to get it if you try to cement it prematurely. *People arrive at their true feelings at their own pace.* Rushing yourself or someone else into feeling something they're unsure of or bending and reshaping yourself to try to be what will get them to commit is the beginning of the end. We know it's exciting and anxiety riddled because you want so badly for it to work out. For something to be "the thing" that fills in the blanks you're leaving open, you have to calm those feelings down. Take your time getting to know not only this person *but also you with this person.* Relationships are like desserts: they are to be savored and enjoyed; otherwise, you rush through them, get a headache, feel sick and wish you hadn't had one in the first place. Besides, what's the rush?

Think about this: when you find the "One" and decide to spend the rest of your life together, barring sudden death, *you're looking at a very long time.* Seriously. That's why people get cold feet before weddings: not because they think they chose the wrong china pattern; it's because **FOREVER IS A LONG F***ING TIME.** Spending the rest of your days with one person is a daunting idea and one that many cannot actually accomplish. The second-guessing about: "Are they the right person for me?"; "Was I really being me when we fell in love or was I being who I thought they wanted me to be?" The reason the divorce rate is so high is because people rush into relationships so quickly and bend and reshape themselves into what they think the other person wants in an effort to nail something down. Then cut to years down the road when the newness has worn off and they realize that they can't stay with this person forever. Or even worse: that they're not that person they pretended to be. **NOT EVERY RELATIONSHIP YOU HAVE IS MEANT TO LAST FOREVER**—that goes for friendships, romances and even family. Maybe that guy you're still hung up on that was the one that got away was only meant to last for two years and that's why it went so wrong in year three.

Even the best relationship is going to have parts that are dull beyond belief and not even noteworthy. The thing about a meaningful relationship is that it will continually change as the two of you change and become more attuned to each other. However, if you rush through the beginning to get to the middle of it, you miss so much of the good stuff that you really need to make a relationship last. Most relationships end because one (or both) people are missing something, longing for something else, someone else, a new set of experiences. Let us make an analogy. Meeting new people, dating new people, having sex with new people, falling in love, feeling lust, anticipation—all of those experiences are like opening a box on Christmas morning. When you're in a long-term relationship, as time goes on you don't get a lot of that "experiencing something new feeling" beyond the big events in your lives. Consequently, when you hit a big lull, rocky, or dull patch you tend crave something different, something new—you want to open a new box. When you race through the good stuff early on in the relationship like a kid tearing through their presents to see what they all are, you don't fully experience opening the boxes in a *memorable way*. So when you're in a bad place in your relationship and could use some reinforcement, you're unable to recall the memories and feelings of that rush of excitement of opening the "first time you kissed" box or the "first time you saw each other naked" box or the "first time you really missed each other" box or the "first time you robbed a bank together" box. It may sound trite, but having those experiences and being hyperaware of them as they're happening is what gets you through tough times in a relationship. It's those experiences *in the beginning* of your relationship that fuel your desire to persevere when things aren't spectacular, instead of abandoning ship to find a new box to open. So if you motor through those moments, the opening of those new boxes, when they're happening they won't resonate as being the profound and excellent experiences that are the building blocks of a lasting union.

The goal is to have a relationship that rocks and lasts forever (which we've established is a very long time), so it's the decision you should be the most discerning and certain of. Think about how much time and thought you put into buying a car. You wouldn't just go to a car dealership, hand him a pile of cash and say, "I'll take the red one." No, you'd want to look at many cars, many models, test drive a few, compare prices, look under the hood, kick the tires and be sure, then double sure, then triple sure that you're making the right choice for you. And buying a car is a decision that you can change every few years! So why would you rush into a relationship without the same deliberation? Look, you're not always going to be in sync with the person you're dating. One of you generally gets in deeper sooner, but don't be afraid to arrive at your emotions at your own pace. Don't mistake having sex as a tool for locking down a relationship. And don't be rushed into being anything other than a Summer Blockbuster Movie! Slow down, be the real you and just be in the moment. The rest will take care of itself.

BUT GREG AND AMIIRA, I'VE GOT QUESTIONS.

BUT DATING ONLINE GOES FAST.

Dear Greg and Amiira,

Okay, so I've been divorced for three years and I'm finally ready to start dating. I meet this guy online and we really hit it off. He sends me funny e-mails that are flirty and cute without being pervy. Finally we decided to meet and go dancing (we both like 70's disco) after about two weeks of corresponding. He's cute, we get along even better in person, and everything seems great except for one thing: he's really anxious to lock down a commitment from me, as though we've been dating this whole time and it's the first time we've met. I can almost feel his panic, and it's turning me off. I never said anything to mislead him or even indicate that I didn't want to date others as well. We have so much in common and I really like him, but I don't want to be pressured into a relationship. That's how my marriage started, and that was a disaster. The flip side is I'm 38 and I don't want to end up alone. Help!

Sophia
Milan, Italy

Dear Panic at the Disco,

Lock this down immediately! Thirty-eight years old? How do you disco with your walker? Are discos even open at 5:30 in the afternoon? Old women like you should hang on to any warm body you can find! Are we making our point? Here's the great thing about your situation: You've been to the dance (literally as well as figuratively) already and this time you want to do it right. Trust that and stop worrying about your age. You set the pace on the Internet or anywhere else and all you've got to do is be communicative with him about how you intend to live your life postdivorce and that you need to take things slowly. If this dude is worth his salt he'll be down with that, and if he's not then he's not the guy you want to dance with anyway. Now go eat your pudding, Grandma.

BUT WHAT IF A SITUATION SPEEDS IT UP?

Dear Greg and Amiira,

I'm dating this guy who is perfect for me, but we've hit a bit of a patch. It started pretty casually, just hanging out a couple times a week at the pub we met at then taking it back to my flat. Things heated up pretty quickly and he started sleeping over a few times a week and everything was great. Here's where it got wonky. His landlord just sold the building he lives in and the new owners just raised his rent excessively, so he can no longer afford to live there. He's got less than a month to find a new flat, so I said that he could move in with me temporarily until he finds one. I thought he'd be excited at the thought since I'm offering a place to stay rent free, and we're already going out so he stays here anyway. But instead of being thrilled he's totally pulled back. What happened?

Sabina
Brussels, Belguim

Dear Rent-Free Romance,

This is a classic case of scaring him off. What happened was you had established a relationship that you were both comfortable with in its frequency of seeing each other and the looseness of future commitment. But by asking him to move in, even temporarily, you made your intentions clear about stepping it up in the future before he was ready to go there. When you propose cohabitation, even out of consideration for his situation, the unspoken caveat is that you're getting more serious, exclusive, and planning a future together. Call him back and tell him that you weren't trying to accelerate the relationship and that you'd love to help him find a place. Everybody likes you when you want to help them move.

BUT WHAT IF I CAN'T HELP MYSELF?

Dear Amiira and Greg,

Doug and I have been on six dates if you include the night we met. I count it because we talked all night and it lasted longer than many of my other first dates have. We just had sex for the first time on our sixth date and I think he likes me as much as I like him. I want him to be my boyfriend and I told him so after we had sex, well, not that bluntly but I initiated the "Where is this thing going?"/"Are you seeing anyone else?"

conversation. He was noncommittal aside from reassuring me that he liked me a lot and that he likes the way things are progressing. What the hell does that mean? I know I shouldn't push him for more, but I don't know if I can help myself. I haven't had a boyfriend in three years and I don't want to lose him, and I don't want to seem desperate either.

Carli

Las Vegas, NV

Dear Borderline Desperation,

Wow, there is a lot going on here. So first things first: not to put too fine a point on it, but we think it's best if you have the "Are you seeing anyone else?" conversation *before* slipping out of your skivvies. It's just healthier. As for the "Where is this thing going?" question, again, if you don't know maybe you shouldn't sleep with this person until you feel comfortable enough that he'll be around afterwards to watch Fallon. Unless this is just a sexual relationship, it's best to ask questions first, then get your "get on" on later. As for his response that he "likes the way things are progressing." You've got your answer. He's not ready to commit, but he's enjoying your sex on the sixth date rule. If you pressure him for more you probably will lose him because people like to arrive at the way they feel because they actually feel it, not because someone's making them feel bad about not feeling it fast enough. Take a deep breath, slow yourself down and try to stay present for the present and not worry about locking down the future. Even if you do end up locking down the relationship, you'll have missed the good stuff that got you there. If you find yourself losing control and wanting to pressure him, then call a friend and ask her to tie you to a tree until the feeling passes.

BUT WHAT IF I'VE ALREADY RUSHED INTO A MARRIAGE?

Dear Greg and Amiira,

I met Jackson at an all day music festival two years ago this summer. It was love at first sight, lust at first sight, completely overwhelming at first sight. By the end of the day we were together, and three months later we got married in Vegas. Things were magical for the first year; everything was perfect, but sometime after that the magic wore off, and it feels like we hardly even know each other. We really love each other and feel like we were destined to be together so we want to make this marriage work. How can we be so close but still feel like complete strangers some days?

Tally
Shreveport, LA

Tally, Tally, Tally,

The problem, you sweet magical little elf, is that you and Jackson never dated so you don't REALLY know each other. The whole reason dating exists is so that people can get to know each other and figure out if there's an attraction and compatibility that is *strong enough* for a long-term commitment. The truth of the matter is that you are married to a relative stranger and had you dated instead of running away to Vegas you would have had a better idea if there was something besides the cosmic connection that you both share or whether or not you can actually live with one another. You rushed through the yummy part and skipped to the middle and now it's not what you expected. We get it. So what do you do? Two things. One: Start dating your husband again. Go out, stay in, spend time together actually TALKING. Find out who you both really are. What your upbringings were like, what your life goals are, and whether you match up for value systems, desire for children, etc. … Two: Go see a professional marriage counselor or therapist and see what someone trained in this field suggests to pull you off the fast track and put you back on the slower path to longevity. After trying these two things you may find that you absolutely had the right instincts about one another or you might find that you aren't compatible at all. Sometimes the cosmos only want us to be together for two months, not a lifetime. And there's nothing wrong with that—we're all guilty of misreading the stars and romantic situations at some point or another.

FROM THE OTHER SIDE OF THE FENCE
BUT HOW SLOW IS TOO SLOW?

Dear Greg and Amiira,
I've been seeing this amazing girl for four weeks now and I'm totally

out of my element. Usually I meet someone, go out once or twice, sleep together, then stay with them for a few months before moving on. I know, not cool, but that has been my pattern up until now. This new girl, Alize, has heard tales about me, so she's been really clear about not wanting to be another notch on my bedpost and wants to take it slow. So we've been dating for a month now and I'm afraid to kiss her. I really like her, more than any other girl I've met, and I don't want to go too fast and make her think that I'm only after sex. How slow is slow enough??

Travis
Bellingham, WA

Dear Snail's Pace,

Man, did you luck out! There is, in our not-so-humble opinion, nothing sexier or better than a woman who knows what she wants and that puts you off your "game." The best advice we can give you is, be honest and forthright with her. Just because she wants to go slow doesn't mean she wants you to not feel sexually towards her. Four weeks in, she might be wondering what's up, so we'd simply tell her in your own way: "Hey, I'm ready for that first kiss whenever you are." Have fun with it and seriously, dude, you will be so happy you guys went this route because you only get the first part of a relationship once, so you might as well make it last.

THE CHICK THAT BLEW IT

I had a crush on this girl from college that I never had the guts to ask out. So years later when I saw her at a college friend's wedding I was determined not to miss my opportunity to go out with her. We started dating and she was as great as I had always imagined she would be, and believe me, I had thought about it a lot over the past nine years. So we're about two months into exclusive dating, I'm seeing her three or four times a week, and we're really starting to get to know each other well. Things are great, she's great, I'm great ... then one night we're having dinner and she's quiet and standoffish. I ask her what's wrong and she says we need to talk about our future. She told me that she's going to be 32 soon and wants to get married and start having kids in the next year or so and if I'm not going to marry her that she doesn't want to see me any more. What?! We've only been dating for two months! Sure, I had thought about her a ton for years but didn't really know her or whether we'd actually be a good match. I told her that it was too soon for me to know. I really was into her and maybe even falling in love with her, but I couldn't tell her for sure two months into dating that we're definitely going to get married and have kids immediately. This was very early on in our relationship, like before meeting each other's friends and family kind of early, and she totally freaked out. It wasn't that she asked—I think it's okay to be clear about what you want—it was her panic about it and demanding that I commit to something as big as marriage before we're even sure we're in love with each other that turned me off. I want to get married, I do, and had she not rushed me with an unrealistic ultimatum we might have gone down that path naturally and maybe even gotten married and had kids in the time frame she wanted, but instead she dumped me. By the way … she's still single and 34 now. How do I know that? Because she recently called to ask if she could see me again, and I felt terrible when I had to tell her that I was engaged.

Aaron

Cleveland, OH

THE CHICK THAT ROCKED IT

Every relationship I've had has gone from zero to living together in like three months flat. Of course, none of those actually lasted because I finally figured out that it takes more than three months to really know someone. Until you've traveled together, nursed the other when they're sick and seen them at least at their semi-worst you have no business moving in together. I've changed apartments and boyfriends five times in the last seven years. So I decided to try something different the next time I got involved with someone who I would self impose an opposite corners rule. That meant no moving in, and sleepovers were on an invite-only basis, not a show up on your doorstep assumption. So when Bradley and I started dating, I took it slow for the first time ever—really slow. Normally my first dates last a week and a half, but this time I let him kiss me goodbye outside the front door. The next time we went out, I got food poisoning and spent the entire night vomiting, which isn't generally a very sexy or romantic second date. Bradley took care of me—I'm talking holding my hair back while I throw up, changing the cold compress on my forehead, renting me movies and going to the deli to get me soup, crackers and ginger ale. The whole weekend he took care of me, only leaving to go home and shower and change clothes. He even did my laundry because I had spewed all over my sheets and pajamas. Bradley and I have been together for almost a year and a half now and I can confidently say that I know him better than anyone else in the world and he holds that same status with me. We've been talking about moving in together soon, which makes me laugh when I think of all the past relationships that I raced through to get to this stage and how little I knew those guys and how those relationships ended as fast as they started. Yesterday we went looking at apartments to see what was out there and we found the perfect place. You know how I knew it was perfect? Because he pulled a ring box out of his pocket and asked me to marry him by the fireplace in the empty living room of our new apartment.

Monica
Brooklyn Heights, NY

FIRST PERSON SINGLE, BY AMIIRA

At this point in my life I can say that I'm an authority on the shelf life of relationships, or rather the authority of what the shelf life *should* have been in hindsight. It's almost embarrassing how poor my judgment was until the age of thirty. There was the boyfriend that I had only intended on going out with for the two months before I moved away, who then followed me across the country, therefore obligating me (in my mind) to stay with him for nearly two years. I knew from the beginning that I wasn't that into being in the relationship but I was young so what's a little time, right? Shelf Life: 2 months. Real Time Spent: 21 months. That'll teach me, though. Not even. How about the guy who had a girlfriend when we met (though he pursued me anyway), who always without fail had overlapping relationships where the new one began before the old one had ended or fizzled out. That's what some might call a giant warning about someone's ability to be faithful and committed to one person. But not to me! I should have probably avoided that guy altogether but I didn't because I was sure he was going to be "The One" and I could change that about him. Surely "Happily Ever After" was just around the corner or some corner if I could just find a freakin' corner to look around. Shelf Life: 6 months. Real Time Spent: 4 ½ years. Gasp! Well at least I'm still pretty young and I've got a couple years before I'm thirty so I'll be fine. Besides, I learn from my mistakes … Oh wait, not when there's best guy friend who's been nothing but supportive during my last breakup that I just adore, who one night after too many Heinekens drunkenly proclaimed his love for me. How could I not give it a try? I do love him … well maybe not like that … but we're such great friends, what could go wrong? Hmmm. I mean, I really wanted it to work because he was so great and it would have been perfect because we were such good friends … but it wasn't great. In fact, it wasn't even great adjacent; it was only mistake adjacent and completely friendship ruining. Shelf Life: 15 (drunken) minutes. Real Time Spent: 1 ½ years. Sweet Linus! What is wrong with me? At that point I really had to sit my own thirty-year-old ass down and say, "What the f***?" When was I going to realize that sometimes lemons are just lemons? You don't have to try to make lemonade out of all of them. There are varying degrees of love and varying degrees of compatibility. Not every guy you like, love or lust after is worth giving up years of your life for, just like not every friend you've ever had will be someone you grow old with. Hell, I couldn't pick my best friend from childhood out of a lineup of three people unless the other two were my children. Same goes for my "soul mate" from college and the guy I went to prom with. It only took me fourteen years of dating to figure that one out, because as we all know, you don't get to be an authority on anything without some serious schooling.

THOUGHTS FROM MAN CITY

We've all been there. You are seeing someone new, it's exciting, there are so many unspoken possibilities in the first few weeks. Everything's going great, and then out of the blue they just up and do it ... They say something that implies a solidifying of the relationship. Like dropping the "I can't wait for my parents to meet my new boyfriend" bomb. Or they start a sentence with: "When we have our own place ..." or "What boy's names do you like? I think Justin is played." You think to yourself, *Why do you have to do that now? We were having so much fun NOT defining it.* There is a time and a place for everything and you know me, I have always been the advocate of asking for what you want in a relationship, but ladies, please! I know that men are guilty of the same thing, so you know how it makes you feel when the shoe is on the other foot. The person you're casually dating and just getting to know suddenly becomes needy, and it freaks you out. Trying to nail down a more defined relationship is not meant to scare guys away, and you'd think we'd be flattered by it, but instead we withdraw because we are not emotionally ready to be there. Everyone comes along at their own speed, and you have to consider that your new person may not be there yet. So when in doubt, wait. You'll know when it's time.

DATING FORTUNE COOKIE

A race is something you try to finish fast. A relationship is something you try to make last.

WORST DATE EVER

Loris and I met at a convention and hit if off immediately. We hung out for the whole weekend and went to every discussion, event and dinner together. It's like we were bonded out of boredom because, let's face it, conventions are D-U-L-L! So at the end of the weekend we exchanged information and decided to stay in touch. She only lived thirty-five miles away, so I called her the week after the convention and asked her to dinner because we had so much fun together. I picked her up at her house and we went to dinner. During dinner she gave me a photo album that she had taken during the convention with a photo of the two of us on the front. She told me that she had looked into transferring to a branch closer to where I lived so it'd be easier for us to hang out. I started to panic but decided to calm down and give her the benefit of the doubt. A few minutes later she got a call on her mobile and told whoever was on the other end of the call that she was at dinner with her boyfriend. When she hung up the phone I told her that we weren't boyfriend/girlfriend and that I considered this to be our first official date. I didn't want to embarrass her but c'mon—hanging out at a convention for three days because you're trapped? She burst into tears, slapped me across the face and yelled that she didn't want to "trap" me any longer. Right in the middle of her air quotes and tears our meals came and I didn't know what to do, so we ate in silence, then I took her home. The thing that sucked is that I liked her and we might have actually gone on to be boyfriend/girlfriend if she had just been on a date with me instead of trying to lock it down.

IT'S JUST A F***ING DATE PT. 2

The journey has to start somewhere. We suggest a date. What's the worst that could happen? At the very least you left the house and went into the world, which is how every great adventure starts unless you have one of those magical wardrobes they write about in books. Now, that doesn't mean every time you go on a date you are going to start a great adventure or even a good one. However, if you go in with an open mind, if you go in not wanting to bail or figure out where the two of you are going to honeymoon, if you go in knowing that any time spent with you is magical, then you might just have a great time.

THE ORIGINAL WORLD FAMOUS WINNER DATER'S WORKBOOK

It's time for personal inventory! Hooray! This is when you take a long look at all your past relationships and identify why you got into them in the first place, how you got into them and why they weren't the right fit. It's important for you to be able to identify any patterns you have with rushing into relationships, compromising who you are to be in them or bending and reshaping yourself to be what someone else wants you to be. It's this type of self-examination that helps you gain the ability to stop repeating patterns and mistakes when entertaining the idea of a relationship. So next time when you find yourself rushing into a relationship and trying to define it quickly you'll be more able to think about what you're doing. Ask yourself: Why you want to be in a relationship so badly? Why are you in such a hurry to lock this thing down? Why are you more concerned with having *any* relationship instead of being sure it's a *good* relationship?

Ready … GO!

PART TWO
CARPE DATEM
SEIZE THE DATE!

WARNING!

The date you are about go on probably won't work out. Most of them don't; that's just life. But if used properly, dates can be one hell of a way to spend an evening and meet another person who, like you, has the hope of someday meeting someone great, so at least you have that in common.

**Dating combined with excessive alcohol intake could prove harmful. Use only as directed.

As your dating "Doctors" we prescribe that you date as much as possible to alleviate the pressure that comes with only going on one date a year.

Welcome to the second part of the *It's Just a F***ing Date!* experience. This is where you learn how to take all your past mistakes, missteps and misconceptions and ignite them in a fiery mass and burn them in a bonfire of "who gives a shit" because they are the past and you are the future.

YOU ARE NOW OFFICIALLY A DATER

You are not a hooker upper or a hanger outer, you are a person who lives and dates at a higher level. When someone is trying to kick down the big steel doors to your prized heart, they will have to make an effort deserving of your exclusive company.

By now you have read and are on your way to mastering the Super Extraordinary Principles For Ultra-Successful Winner Dating. You now know there are a lot of factors that influence any dating situation from how you approach dating (Does it give you hives, arrhythmia, verbal diarrhea?), how you prepare yourself (Do you need a shot of whiskey before you open the front door?), to how to behave (Ladylike always trumps high fives and beer farts.) and what to wear on the date (Panties yes, Crocs no!). What exactly are permissible topics on a first date (Stay away from bodily functions, family dysfunction and ex-boyfriends.)? Should you worry about waxing and lingerie (Always, because you never know when you're going to be in a car accident and they're going to be seen. But it's *your* little secret.)? What's he thinking when he does X, Y & Z (Who f***ing cares! What are YOU thinking when he does X, Y & Z?)? This next part of our excellent tome is dedicated to how to get dates and how to go on them.

Dating is like going on Space Mountain for the first time. Once you commit to doing it and strap yourself in, you have no idea what's going to happen. Scary, right? Sure, but the other thing it can be is a blast or even a scary blast. Dating is supposed to be fun or at least relatively painless, but somehow we've made dating the villain or the enemy in the quest to find love.

Yes, there can be a degree of fear, dread even, when you're faced with the prospect of finding someone worthy of dating in the first place (which isn't the easiest thing to do), then pile on the factors of getting them to notice you back, going out on a date, playing your cards right, not having sex too soon or freaking each other out, not future-projecting your wedding plans or reacting to scenarios that haven't and may never happen. Then there's the rejection, ohhhh the unrelenting sting of the rejection that tortures you while it dissolves your self-esteem like butter on hot toast. It's a complete maelstrom: a whirlpool of emotion and confusion that stays and messes with your head indefinitely. Then why do you put up with it? Why should you put up with it? The maelstrom only happens because you do it to yourself. We call it Self Emotional Terrorism. When you put that kind of pressure on anything, dating included, it's not going to be fun. How could it be when It's Just a F***ing Date? Why not take each challenge as it presents itself instead of trying to figure them all out before you've left the house? Heck, why even view it as a challenge instead of an opportunity? Dating is an opportunity to get to know another human being for all their quirks and shining glory. How is that not a good time? Even a shitty date makes for a good story the next day over coffee with your posse.

We know that it's easier said than done ... or is it? Here's a preview of what lies ahead to guide you on your quest for getting dates, going on dates, and not blowing it.

THE ESSENCE OF KEEPING IT COOL, KNOWN AS ZEN AND THE ART OF CARPE DATEM

Essence #1 There Is No One Place to Meet Guys
Where the boys are

Essence #2 The Power Of Suggestion
How to get asked out

BONUS SECTION! INTERNET DATE-TACULAR!
Tickling the keypad

Essence #3 It's Just a F***ing First Date!
How to be a great first date and how to have one

Essence #4 First Date Follow-Up
Communication and the RIGHT next move

Essence #5 2nd Date And Beyond
Pacing your dates and the formula for success

Essence #6 Sexclusivity
Getting it on and locking it down

Not to put too fine a point on it, but dating is all we have for the next hundred years until we're all assigned a barcode on our silver jumpsuits that correlates with our preselected mate. By the way, in the future we all live on the space station, but at least we get to wear silver jumpsuits. Like we've mentioned before, most dates you go on won't work out just like most relationships won't work out … UNTIL THE ONE THAT DOES. But that's the one that everyone is searching for and if you didn't know in your heart that when you find your person, your "One," that every single thing you've gone through and endured would be worth it, you'd have given up already. Finding the One is worth it every day of the week and twice on Sunday.

That's why we say CARPE DATEM! SEIZE THE DATE!

ESSENCE # 1
THERE IS NO ONE PLACE
TO MEET GUYS

Where the Boys Are

"There's no one out there to date." And "*(insert your town's name, your state's name, country's, school's or continent's)* is the worst place to date." Those are the two most common complaints that we've heard from all the Singles we've encountered since we first started writing relationship books. So either dating on the other planets is a piece of cake or finding someone to date is a universal problem. (We're betting our chips on the latter.) Here's the good and bad news: There Is No **One** Good Place To Meet Someone. Everywhere there are people is a good place to meet a potential date. Seriously, even the morgue could be a good place if the forensics guy was hot and you caught each other's eye. It isn't about where you go, because there are men everywhere you go and look … except at women-only venues like the ladies room and La Leche League, and who wants to date the guy at the breastfeeding meetings? These guys you see nearly everywhere you go in life are looking to meet you too. Besides, it's less about "where" than you think.

Maybe if you've been paying attention you know that making a connection or having an impact is more about *WHO* you are when you're there, than *WHERE* you are. Who you are pulls the focus of others and either keeps it or dismisses it. Our motto is: why be dull or drab when you could be sparkly?

Let's expand on that concept because it draws upon a number of the Principal Principles of Ultra-Successful Winner

Dating. Who you are when you go anywhere in the world (meaning what you project to others) will determine what types of people you will attract and how people respond to you. The goal is to have people respond to you, be drawn to you and be curious about you. So once you've put all the Principles of Ultra-Successful Winner Dating into effect you will start attracting new people. If you like yourself and know you're worthy you'll carry yourself with an air of confidence, which is SPARKLY. If you have a life that is buoyant, fulfilling and interesting you'll exude that kind of energy, an energy that reads as SPARKLY. When you've taken the time to look really good from your head to your toes and in between you'll radiate the magnetism of a woman completely self-possessed who has some serious standards and is, you guessed it, SPARKLY. Let's be real: you don't want to meet just *anyone* because just anyone won't do; otherwise, you would have settled for the guy that threw up on you at the fair in high school. You want to meet someone who values himself as much as you value yourself (another Ultra-Successful Winner Dater type of guy, if you will) that you might have something in common or share an interest with, right?

Now that you know *WHO* you need to be when you go out (a radiant and together superhot lady who likes herself, knows her worth and lives a life that rocks) we need to get back to the *WHERE* you should be going. If you want to meet someone who you share an interest with, you have to narrow down where the best places for you to meet potential suitors would be out of all the places available to you to meet the male of the species on this earth. There are the obvious ideas, like to go to the park or join a hiking group if you love the outdoors and want to meet a fellow outdoorsman. Or hit the galleries and museums if you want to find an art lover like yourself. Sure, these are valid (if not predictable) suggestions, but we think you should **get specific with who you are and where you will shine the brightest when deciding where to go to meet a great guy**. When you're somewhere that you truly are excited about being or that you connect with on a *deeper* level, you are more likely to be comfortable, confident and magnetic. All of which are spectacularly winning assets when it comes to attracting future dates. So think about it: Where do you love being? What do you love doing? Where are you the best version of you (besides at home where there aren't other potential human beings to date)? Those are the places that you are most likely to be a person that attracts and intrigues others and meet someone you will connect with. Do you get what we're talking about?

Do you love Mumford & Sons? Does their music move you at the core of your being? Then go to Mumford & Sons concerts where there will be other people that connect to their music and where you'll most certainly be looking foxy, exuding joy and being the most exotic and sparkly you that you are. If you happen to meet someone at the Mumford & Sons show then you already know you have one thing in common that you can have a full conversation about. Or if you're a diehard supporter for the environment then get involved and *stay* involved with its causes, fundraisers or protests on a regular basis and go meet some other activists. Even if all the activists you meet that are appealing to you are women, you still win because women sometimes have male friends and brothers, as it turns out. If you like a woman, you'll probably like her male friends and siblings and you can ask her to hook you up.

Sure, you can go to bars and nightclubs if that's where you feel great, but generally the people going to bars and nightclubs aren't there looking for long-term relationships as much as someone to hook up, hang out or have sex with. Not to mention that anywhere where drinking is the main activity offered is dangerous non-dating territory. C'mon people, we've discussed this already! The places you go, your venues, send a message to the people around you because they're probably at those same venues for similar reasons. A bar says *I like drinking and having some casual, letting-off-some-steam fun.* A nightclub says *I like dancing, music, drinking, and casual racy fun.* Whole Foods says *I'm serious about the planet and my body. I try to surround myself with the best options for me and I put a lot of thought into it ... and I'm probably a yoga enthusiast.* Jiffy Lube says *I can handle my own affairs and am a self-sufficient woman who looks very cute in her casual weekend car maintenance attire.*

All right, we know who you need to be when you're out in the world to attract guys and where you should go to narrow the field of guys; now it's up to you to meet them. Not every guy you want to approach you will. It's sad but true ...mind control is still not perfected. So there are times when it's up to you to break the ice and pull the focus over to your "Sparklyness" or whatever you want to call your badass self. Sure, you can see a guy you want to meet and go over and introduce yourself and hope for conversation that makes him notice that there's something cool about you. But why not see a guy you want to meet and just be sparkly up front with the way you meet him?

LET US SHOW YOU HOW IT'S DONE

Setting: You're at a restaurant. He's cute but engaged in conversation with his buddies and doesn't notice you.

Possibly awkward introduction:

"Good burgers, huh? I'm Jen, by the way."

(Now, the reason this could be awkward is that he may not want to be interrupted and be dismissive to you as a result.)

Sparkly introduction:

"Can I borrow your ketchup?"

(Wait for ketchup.)

"Can I borrow a French fry to go with it?"

(Wait for French fry and smile or laugh from cute guy that appreciates how clever you are and is pleased to be interrupted by such.)

"Thanks. You can put it on my tab. My name's Jen."

(Hello, sparkly lady!)

The ketchup episode laid out for you above could be a lady trying to pick up a guy OR it could just be a confident, flirty lady that wanted a French fry and can be played off as either. There's always a way to stand out without being too obvious and always a way to blend in while still being sparkly. It takes work at first, but once you get the hang of it, it becomes second nature. Then it's like bees to honey.

The other thing you need to know is that patience and persistence are part of the equation to meeting quality guys. Just because "he" wasn't at the place you went looking for him once doesn't mean he won't be there next time. So be consistent about going to places that make it easy for you to be the best you. Find lots of places where you are the best, brightest, and most confident you and get out often!

Then there's the Internet! Which is like a twenty-four-hour international singles mixer where the possibilities for meeting people are right there if you have the patience to point and click your way through the room. There are specific dating sites, special interest sites, chat rooms and lifestyle sites all in an effort to connect people. If you put up a Facebook page or join a dating website it's hard *not* to meet people, but weeding through and nurturing cyber relationships takes a lot of attention. The time commitment alone can be the downside of looking solely to the Internet to meet people. The upside being that you can reach masses of people and the convenience of being able to window-shop for love in your pajamas. We advise, nay, WE STRONGLY INSIST that the Internet alone should not make up your social life or interactions.

SURROUNDED BY SINGLE MEN, BY AMIIRA

Another thing to think about when looking for potential dates is playing the odds. Where would you stand out? In addition to going to places where you shine because you are in your element, how about trying places where you will be exotic? I want to share the story of when I was asked out on the most dates in my life because I stood out and was exotic and sparkly. When I was single I decided to take golf lessons. I did not take golf lessons to meet men but rather because I wanted to learn how to play golf. Most of the men in my line of work played golf and had their business meetings over a round of golf, which seemed spectacular to me, and I wanted to get in on that action. Getting to be outside playing a three- to six-hour round of golf instead of being in the office was very appealing to a girl like me who prefers basking in the sunlight over the fluorescents. Anyway, I started taking golf lessons from a lovely old man named Ed who reminded me of my Granddaddy. I loved my golf lessons because Ed was both amusing and wise and for whatever reason, working on my golf swing was a very Zen experience that I came to crave. There was a stillness to the time during my golf lessons that was in complete contrast to every other aspect of my life. Basically, my golf lessons were my time for me where everything else in my head disappeared and I was content and concentrating on the now. I was living in the moment with purpose. I didn't notice it at first because I was truly just working on my swing, learning the clubs and seeing what I could do with them, but men would gather to watch my golf lesson. Or rather watch me take my lesson, then wait for it to be over so they could chat me up. Ed noticed and would tell them to get lost, not to bother me because he was like my Granddaddy and he didn't need a bunch of lookie-loos interrupting our time together. The point I'm trying to make is that I stood out and was exotic and sparkly at the golf club for a couple of reasons. Firstly, I was usually the only woman at the driving range or one of maybe three on a busy weekend compared to the nearly hundred men that would pass through during my hour there. Secondly, I had a purpose and wasn't easily distracted from it because I truly enjoyed what I was doing and had the desire and focus to get better at it. Thirdly, I wasn't trolling for dates, which probably read the same as playing hard to get. Since I was at a sporting venue, you can imagine that there were men that like a challenge there, and my disinterest was challenging to them. Needless to say, I have never been asked out on more dates in my entire life. Maybe it was because I had it going on, or maybe it was because I was the only girl there and guys couldn't believe their luck to find a girl that likes golf! Either way, I was exotic and sparkly and therefore brightened the place (which is quite an accomplishment for the outdoors), and all the young dudes seemed to notice.

THE NEW LAW OF ATTRACTION, BY GREG

Here's what I know about attraction: It really isn't just about looks. Human beings give off a vibe when they are happy and they are, I believe, happiest when they are closest to the dream, whatever that may be for them. I know I'm a guy, but let me share this with you and see if it resonates or at least makes sense. From the time I was old enough to know they existed, I loved women. Almost every action I took from the age of four on was in an effort to get closer to them. Now, I've always been a pretty good student of life but not a great student of me. Here's an example: When I was growing up and you wanted the girl, you could do no better than play sports. Football especially was a really great way to get noticed so, naturally, I played football. I was horrible at it—I mean *really* bad. Needless to say, I didn't do so well with the ladies. But I continued down this path because I didn't understand that it wasn't football that got the girls but how it made those who played it well feel and appear. The girls didn't just like Todd Leitz because he was dead sexy and played football; they liked him because he liked himself and loved being good at football. Joe Malatesta was great looking too, but he couldn't catch a pass. No chicks for Joe. It wasn't until I took a theatre class in college to fill an arts requirement that I began to understand this idea of who you are when you are closer to your dream. My mother always encouraged me to get involved in theatre because she thought I was funny. I always thought that theatre was weak and for pussies. Well, oddly enough, I excelled at theatre and I'm not weak nor am I a pussy, and suddenly there were girls. I was at a place maybe for the first time in my life where I was comfortable in my skin, and it showed. I didn't know it yet, but I was getting closer to my dream. Later that year I was asked to join a band. More girls. Life was grand; I was more me than I'd ever been. Then tragedy struck. I graduated and moved to San Francisco. No more band, no more acting, much more waiting tables and NO GIRLS. Then my mom calls and tells me about an audition for an improvisational comedy group. So I audition, I get asked to join, and two weeks into it one of the other members of the group suggests I try stand-up comedy. I try it, I like it and suddenly there are GIRLS! Now when I say girls, I'm not talking about just sex, I'm saying that is when I was the most attractive to them. When they would say "yes" to me asking them out and when I handled rejection better because I knew what they were missing out on when they said "No." Whatever my relationship with myself was directly reflected in my relationships with others. And my relationship with myself corresponded with my proximity to my dream life. Now, my dream was to be a great stand-up, so it's no surprise I met my wife after taping my first HBO special. I'm not saying I'm a great stand-up; I'm saying I was in this world trying to accomplish what I think I was put here to do. That made me happy, and so my sense of place and purpose made me attractive to the girl of my dreams. It really is a matter of sorting out what your dream is. It's there in your head, that thing that if you could wave a magic wand and do you would do in a heartbeat. *That's* the person you are waiting to become and that's the person you need to be or on the path to becoming to attract the right person to you. If you attract someone while *not* in pursuit of the dream and then you suddenly want to go get it they may not want to come with you, or worse, try and stop you. Go for the dream first.

LOVE IN THE BREAKROOM

"What if the place I am my best is at the office, but interoffice dating is forbidden?" That's a good question, and our answer may surprise you a bit. We just think it's a bad idea to rule out any place where a love connection could be made. (Okay, maybe prison.) Three of the happiest couples we know met at work, including Greg's parents. Now, we don't want you to get fired or make foolish choices with your career just because the person in the next cubicle has a nice butt. However, we are loathe to tell you to rule out the work environment as a place to find someone to date. Where else are you going to find someone with the same passion for blacksmithery than at your job at the blacksmith place where you do your blacksmithing? You get the point. When you meet through work, there's already an ease and commonality because you have work and coworkers in common. You have the work place to agree, disagree or argue about, and you have the opportunity to spend a lot of time getting to know one another as friends and coworkers. While we think that the workplace is a good place to meet people, you have to understand what ultimately is at stake … your job. How do you feel about the possibility of having to work with your ex, because that COULD happen? It's a slippery slope, but it doesn't mean it's not worth trying to ski it for the right person. It really comes down to what's more important: taking a chance that this might be your person (The One) or job stability.

Here are some tips to help you really decide if this guy or gal is worth risking your job and sanity over, as well as some suggestions about pursuing love in the workplace. These are offered in hopes that you won't be one of the many burned by a fiery office romance.

> Does your workplace have a policy against interoffice dating, and what are the consequences? Is it frowned upon, or will you be terminated? There is a sliding scale depending on your company as to what the feeling is about dating among the ranks, and probably another hurdle to get over which is, how does your direct boss feel about it? Is it a respect killer? Meaning will they lose all respect for you, treat you differently or ultimately make being at work a bummer?

> How important is your work or this job? Is this a career-making job for you, just a stepping-stone in the scheme of things, or simply a place where you punch the clock? This evaluation plays a big part in your decision as well. If it's a career maker you might want to hold off until he or she goes to another company. Perhaps you can even talk to your supervisor about it. Maybe you can transfer

to the Starbucks across the street or maybe you'll never work for the company again and couldn't give a shit because this person is worth finding a new job for.

Do you think this person is super hot, or is this THE person that you will always regret not having taken the chance for? Sometimes it's hard to really tell the difference because the office is like a suspended reality. Working together is almost like dating because you get to spend a ton of time together, talk constantly and really get to know each other within the confines of work. Certainly you can grow close to a workmate and the line can get blurry as to what you feel for them. When you are coworkers you create an intimacy, a bond, a relationship that has its own private jokes and shorthand. That in itself can feel really confusing, and you may not be able to tell if you're having a crush or falling in love. Just because you work well as workmates doesn't mean you'll work in the real world or under the pressure and scrutiny of your coworkers and bosses.

If you've decided to throw caution to the copier and go for it, here's some guidelines to consider.

Be discreet and keep it on the DL (that's "Down Low" for those of you untouched by popular culture). Respect each other's jobs and reputation. There is no need for Shari in the next cubicle to know what kind of boxers he sleeps in.

Take it off campus. Keep the office a professional place and do your dating and heavy petting after-hours.

Get clarity from each other. Is this a fling or a

relationship? Know what you're getting into, because the fallout is big when you have to see your ex at work every day and watch them date someone else.

Ask yourself: Is this exciting because it's forbidden or because you're crazy about this person? If you don't know the answer, you're doing it for the wrong reasons.

THAT'S JUST YOU LOOKING FOR A LOOPHOLE

Why do I have to go out when I can shop online for men in my sweats? Because life is meant to be lived, not watched on a tiny screen. Besides, since you are rocking it with so many men online, going out should be even more fun. Who knows what awesome guy you'll attract when you are *not* looking for someone and are out of your sweats. We understand the appeal of not having to try or really put yourself out there because damn it that shit is hard! But take it from us, when all is said and done you won't wish you'd spent more time sitting at home instead of being face-to-face with another human being. Most importantly, and here's the real truth, *you can't get to know a person until you are actually with them.* There is no better advertisement for you than the way you walk into a room or the sound of your laugh. Even the way you burp after you chug a beer is far more enticing than reading that you really wish you could meet Rihanna on your Twitter feed. Not to mention that you'd have a better chance of meeting Rihanna if you'd just leave the house.

CARPE DATEM ROCK'EM SOCK'EM SUPERBOOK

It's time to figure out where you should be going to meet prospective dates. Hopefully you've been thinking about the things we've said along the chapter and doing some real searching about where you shine the brightest. Now, we all know that you can find love in both the most random and predictable places and that ultimately it's not something you can control or will into being. But we also know that you can't lose by honoring yourself and being the best you by looking your best, then going to places where you project confidence and happiness. Let's figure out where that is.

List the five environments that you feel the best in. (Be specific. Is it walking down Fifth Avenue in the bustling city at twilight? By the ocean on an absurdly hot day?)

1.

2.

3.

4.

5.

List the five places that you can go that you've always wanted to go. (This can be a restaurant, park, exhibit or an actual journey.)

1.

2.

3.

4.

5.

List the five places in your city that you love the most.

1.

2.

3.

4.

5.

List the five things you wished you had done that you haven't done yet. (Skydiving? Eating Sushi? Eating Sushi while skydiving?)

1.

2.

3.

4.

5.

Now get dolled up and go out and get 'em!

ESSENCE #2
THE POWER OF SUGGESTION

How to Get Asked Out

While it would be great if there were no more hurdles now that you've figured out *where* you should be going, *who* you should be when you get there, and *how* to meet the right kind of guy, we're far from done. We don't know if you've noticed, but guys aren't stampeding down the doors to ask ladies out on dates these days. Is it really that much easier to ask women to hang out or hook up than it is to ask them on a date? Apparently so. Muttering something along the lines of "We're all going down to Fuzzy Jacks for some Spud Duds, Spicy Knuckles and Beer Biscuits" has a difficulty degree of negative five while mustering up the cojones to say, "How about having dinner with me this Friday?" is evidently a considerably more complicated challenge. As we explained in the very first chapter of this book, an invitation to hang out or hook up lowers the expectations on both sides considerably. Why? Because the subtext of a hang out is: "You can come or not come ... whatever." Whatever? Really? You want to spend your time with someone whose feeling about you is kind of whatever? We don't think so. The other thing about hanging out or hooking up is that guys use it as an opportunity to sample your company to determine whether or not they like you enough to go out with you under more official circumstances. That means the guy feels like he's not totally putting himself out there, making himself vulnerable to rejection (even if his palms are sweating the whole time), PLUS the woman's expectation of what the actual get-together means are much lower. Less threat, less commitment, vague definition—it's a completely winning formula for a guy. But it's literally an audition for the lady, which is NOT winning for the lady. Women like definition; they like to know what the game is, what's going on, who the players are, and where they stand. That's why women who want to *date* need to not only stop accepting casual suggestions of hanging out and hooking up, but also need to make dating an easier prospect for men to get their head around. It's up to you to embody the **It's Just a Date!** philosophy (*letting go of the whole process but not letting go of you*) and remove the pressure and expectation from the situation so that guys can look at dating as a good thing instead of with trepidation. Otherwise, men will continue to NOT ask women out, and women will continue to do the heavy lifting or even worse, settling for quasi dating on a man's terms. Like the Beyoncé song says, "Who runs the world? Girls!"

Look, not every guy you want to ask you out will. Some won't be interested, some will be too shy, some would rather not-date you because of a mild allergy to even *that* small form of commitment. That goes for when you're standing in the same room and when you're online. Then what? Should you give him your phone number? Hand him your business card? Write down your e-mail or Facebook page? NO. Really. NO. We're not kidding. Guys like the chase. Therefore, the goal is to make him ASK for those things. Therefore, it's up to you to **Give The Right Signals** (see box). Make asking you out easy and inviting when you find yourself in a situation where the guy you want to make a move is being a pussy and not making the move. As we talked about in the last chapter, you can meet whoever you want once you've engaged in some level of conversation or short distance flirting, but you may have to CREATE those opportunities for yourself, because as we've mentioned before … guys can be lame. When necessary, you need to present the idea of going on a date with you as an incredibly enticing opportunity that he wouldn't want to pass up. How do you accomplish that? By being confident, sparkly and *possibly* willing to find a place in your schedule for him.

LET US SHOW YOU HOW IT'S DONE.

Example:

Say a guy is hinting at the idea that you should hang out sometime but not asking you out. Instead of agreeing to an undefined possible future get-together, you give him specific choices.

"Ohhh, sorry. I'm booked through the next millennium for hang outs, but I'd be available for a date either Thursday for dinner or brunch on Saturday. After that I may be going out of town on a top secret assignment, so those are really my only free days."

If he's hesitant to nail down a date, then either he's actually propositioning you for the possibility of sex or not that interested and using the "hang out" idea as a way to wrap up the conversation so he can move on.

Example:

You're at a party and he's across the room, occasionally glancing your way. If he doesn't ever come over to you, even after you've shot him a number of smiles and flirty glances, you wave him over (as in "come here"). If he doesn't come then you have your answer; if he does make the journey across the room, you offer something along the lines of …

"Hey, handsome, I couldn't tell if you were looking over here because you wanted to talk to me or because there's a clock somewhere behind me. So I thought I'd give you the opportunity to either ask me out or get a better look at the time."

He'll either be relieved at your humor or totally freaked out. Both give you an equally good reason to giggle with sparkly confidence.

Example:

You're talking to a bunch of guys, all of whom you're having fun with, but none of whom are asking you out.

"It's too bad that all of you are cute and funny but none of you have asked me out, because I have an extra ticket to the Lakers game that I'll have to waste on someone else."

By the way, having tickets to a sporting event is an easy way to get asked out. Hell, it'd be worth you investing in season tickets with a girlfriend. You could go together because it's fun (plus, there's always single guys there), give some tickets away and use the tickets to the really good games to get dates!

Example:

You're anywhere with a guy who you wants to ask you out.

"You know what I think? I think you should ask me on a date to go see Spider-Man 7 (or whatever the hot movie that's opening that week is) Saturday night."

Sometimes the power of suggestion isn't subtle, but what we're looking for is getting asked out in advance on an actual date.

Example:

You're online dating and you see a guy whose profile you like because he's also a huge Local Natives fan and whose photo you REALLY like, but he hasn't winked or e-mailed you. So you e-mail him.

"Hey there. How do I know you? Were you the guy in the fourteenth row of the Local Natives show that switched seats with me so I wasn't behind the tall guy, or did we go to high school together? (If it's the latter, are you still friends with Travis?)"

Now, clearly this is a load of crap, but you're looking for a response in a wasteland of unanswered e-mails, and this will pique his interest for two reasons. First, that you were at Local Natives and had great seats so you're clearly hooked up and second, everyone went to school with someone who might have been named Travis, so he'll think it's possible. Once he emails back you can discover that he's not the same guy you met/went to high school with, but by then hopefully you'll have struck up a correspondence. Sorry ladies, we don't mean to encourage dishonesty, but sometimes fishing is fishing, and there's got to be bait.

These are a few examples of ways to make asking you out easy for a guy, and certainly some guys will bite at the opportunity and others will pass. SO WHAT?! The guys that pass aren't right for you anyway, and the ones that bite might not be either. Dating is a numbers game, and you have to go out with a number of frogs before you find a prince.

THE PLAYS

There are only a few options available to you if a guy doesn't ask you out. You can:

Figure he's not interested and move on with your life. Which by all means is a fine option to go with, because who wants to be with a guy that doesn't even have enough balls to ask a girl out? If you've made eye contact, smiled in his general direction, or undressed him with your eyes and he's not coming over, he's either got a girlfriend, might be gay or is just lazy. None of which are good enough for you!

Ask him out on a date. To that Amiira says, "Hell no you don't!" Just because you're an independent woman that can take charge of a situation and go for what you want doesn't mean that you can change the fact that men like to do the chasing, and when women take that away from them by being the aggressor, they lose interest quickly. So you may get your date but you probably won't get your man.

Make him a one time only offer. This is THE GREAT DATING LOOPHOLE that we've come up with that allows women to participate in their dating lives without having to do the asking. It goes like this: Say there's a guy that you're hot for that's not making the moves on you. You saunter up to him, give him a tap on the shoulder, and with a coy yet confident delivery let him know that you have a one time only offer for him. Tell him, "There's a five-minute window of opportunity that's opening right now for you to ask me out. After that I can't guarantee that it will ever come around again." This flirty offer delivers the same message as asking a guy out on a date because it lets him know that you'd like to go out with him but makes you seem confident, intriguing, and actually still makes him do the asking.

Don't take it all so seriously. It's Just a F***ing Date! and if he doesn't ask you out on one then you're probably not missing much and he's not the guy for you.

ASKING MEN OUT, BY GREG

Can women ask men out? I have been asked this question since the first hour *He's Just Not That Into You* came out. The reason being is that in that book I asserted that if a guy is into you, he WILL ask you out. That's what *I* believe. *I* was raised to ask women out; my friends were raised to ask women out. THE POWERS THAT BE, SCIENCE OR OTHERWISE, MADE YOU PRETTY SO WE'D CHASE YOU AROUND. In fact, I can't imagine any dad in this or any country sitting in their young son's bedroom saying, "Just look pretty the next time you see her at the library and maybe she'll ask you out." Now, that being said, I'm also not saying it's right. It just is. I understand how infuriating this all is, but I didn't set it up; we are ALL doing battle with history and gender roles. We'd love for the shoe to be on the other foot. Asking girls out is f***ing terrifying! But since women have periods and give birth, maybe we should have the responsibility of doing **one thing** that's hard. Does all this mean women shouldn't ask men out? No. That's ridiculous. Women have minds of their own. But it does mean that *MEN KNOW THAT THEY ARE SUPPOSED TO ASK YOU OUT* and that *I* think men are better as well as more invested when they are in pursuit. That was the truth for me. However, I would hate to encourage someone not to participate in his or her own life or be a victim of circumstance. If you think asking a man out will make your life better, then how could I possibly tell you not to? But if you were my sister, I'd strongly encourage you to flirt heavily first, nudge him a bit and if he doesn't take the bait then he's just not that ...

THE RIGHT SIGNALS, BY AMIIRA

Clearly, when you're out in the world meeting these guys that haven't got the ability to string together an invitation to dinner, there's a part you play in the equation. That part is roadblock or doorway. The roadblock shuts down the possibilities for the approach, whereas the doorway opens to it. Now, being approachable doesn't mean you're easy, it just means you're receptive. Sending the right signals to let a guy know that approaching you is a winning idea is all about finesse.

LOOKS

Obviously, it helps to look good and be your sparkly yummy self because we now accept that men are visual creatures and as such they respond to visual cues. That means a hint of skin, be it *slight* cleavage, legs, feet (sorry flat lovers, but men respond to a strappy heel even if you're tall), tattooed shoulder, back, neck ... just something that reminds them that you're a woman. Also, gloss those lips, do something with your hair, and wear something that alludes to the shape of your body; don't hide it in the equivalent of a giant sack. Even if you're a bigger lady, wearing big clothes makes you look bigger; it doesn't hide you, and STOP HIDING anyway! In this day and age, there are flattering affordable clothes for every body type out there, but you have to go find them. The idea is to subtly provoke a sexual response from men, and when I say response I'm talking about a flicker of thought, not an erection.

MAKE EYE CONTACT

If there's a guy you fancy, look him in the eye. Make eye contact and hold eye contact for a moment or two before looking away. Don't have a staring match, but don't avoid holding his gaze. The frequency and duration of your glances in his direction, your actual eye contact, and your holding his gaze is like a conversation the two of you are having with your eyes. This eye conversation (sometimes referred to as eye-f***ing) can determine whether he ultimately asks you out on a date or tries to get you in the coat closet, so be careful with those laser beams 'cause they can get you into real trouble! I like playing it kind of cool and trying to draw out the eye conversation because it's a great flirting device and speaks volumes without having to say a word. Try something like ... glance, look away (to the side, not down), glance back, catch his eyes—hold for two seconds, then smile, look away, catch his eyes, hold for four seconds with lips pursed in a slight grin but not smiling, pull shoulders down and back slightly to emphasize your assets and lower head deliberately for a moment, then return to his gaze. Be small yet deliberate with your movements so you appear to be completely confident and controlled yet intrigued, not giggly like you can't believe he's actually looking at you. Repeat as necessary until he engages further.

FLIRTING

What's more fun than flirting? Almost nothing. While flirting comes naturally to some, it is a skill that must be developed by many. The point of flirting is to connect with him in a playful way that creates a sense of familiarity and makes him want to spend more time with you. Flirting is not only a huge aphrodisiac; it's almost addictive. The positive attention of flirting feels awesome and makes you want more. Flirting is making eye contact as described above, it's being playful and suggestive without being too sexual, it's teasing and good-hearted kidding, it's using touch in an intimate way to emphasize your interest. Flirting is hard to describe, so for reference think Julia Roberts whenever she's on David Letterman.

BODY LANGUAGE

Be open ... literally. Don't hunch down or over; instead, throw your shoulders back, chin up, and put a pleased look on your face. Be open and receptive to the approach. Be the bright spot in any room and the most inviting person to talk to. Use your hands to gesticulate, entice and emphasize, but don't overdo it. You want to invite interest without seeming like you're seeking attention. A person's body language is a representation of how they feel and who they are. If you want to be approached, then make sure your body language says that it's safe to engage. That goes for you too, Goth girl!

ENGAGING HIM

Be interested and interesting. Draw him in with the attention you give him and how well you listen. Ask questions about his life, work, interests, the political climate, the movie of the year, the difference between geckos and iguanas. Whatever! Just be able to talk and don't be a bore. Again, this is all about your energy and connecting in an intriguing yet familiar way. Have something to talk about in case he isn't the best conversationalist. Is there a funny thing that happened to you, a bet you're trying to settle that he can weigh in on, or a new band that you think everyone in the world should hear? Trying to find something in common besides a sexual attraction is the difference between being a girl he wants to make out with and being a girl he asks out on a date. If you're having trouble engaging him, then maybe you don't want to go out with him anyway. Besides, what would you talk about for an hour over dinner if you can't get a conversation off the ground now?

WHAT TO SAY

Now all you need to know is how to close the deal and how to decline an unwanted invitation with the finesse of an Ultra-Successful Winner Dater. Here are a few of my favorite phrases to encourage a guy to ask you out if he's not taking the initiative. For me it's the preferred method to doing the asking yourself because it basically sends the same message while making yourself seem smart, confident, flirty, and most importantly— *still a challenge*. You will have better success if you're able to deliver these lines in a confident yet flirty way.

"I only ever get asked out by funny guys but never funny **and** handsome ones like you."

"Did you want to ask me something? It seems like you were thinking about asking me something, like if I liked Chinese food and was available for dinner on Friday?"

"As much as I'd like to hang out with you, hanging out is for amateurs and I've already turned pro. I can only go on dates now, but you know where to find me if you ever get decide to turn pro too."

"I'm going to be over here with my friends in case you wanted to come over and ask me out."

"I don't care how charming you are, I'm not going to go out with you so don't even try to persuade me."

HOW TO DECLINE A DATE

There are going to be guys that ask you out that you don't want to go out with. It just happens and it sucks to have to reject another human being. So before you do, you should ask yourself why you don't want to go out with them. Always remember that the art of Ultra-Successful Winner Dating is not typecasting people and narrowing your field.

"You seem like a very cool guy, but I can't date anyone that I feel brotherly towards. But I love my brother very much, so please take that as a compliment."

"That's so funny that you asked me out because I was just thinking I'd like to set you up with one of my friends. If you like me you'll really like her."

"I can't go out with nice guys until I stop my 'dating assholes' phase."

"I'd be doing a disservice to the next spectacular lady you ask out by wasting your time now when I'm still a bit messed up from my last go-around."

"I'm starting a thirty-day detox cleanse tomorrow so I can't do anything but drink green juice and meditate. Try me in a month." Then if he tries you in a month you really should give him a shot.

Remember, giving the right signals is a key component to getting asked out on a date. The sooner you master how to send them, the sooner you can reap the rewards, so get busy!

THE NEW LAWS OF ATTRACTION, BY GREG

Give us an opening.

If you are a guy and you are not on fire or Channing Tatum, most of you women don't look at us. You just don't. Or if you do it's so subtle that we're quite sure it was a mistake. I've even talked to my best-looking guy friends about this, so I knew it wasn't just me, and they all agree it's very hard to tell if you are interested in us. Which makes it even more difficult to ask you out. We have the same self-confidence issues you have; we are only flesh and beer, so it would be great to know you've noticed us. If you don't smile at us, how are we supposed to know it's okay to talk to you or that you are not on your way to see your boyfriend? This probably hasn't kept some of us from coming up to you at the bar, Starbucks, or a laundromat and bugging the shit out of you. Maybe that's the problem … some creepy, persistent dude wrecked it for the rest of us. But all I keep hearing is thatno one is asking you out. So help us out, ladies. Throw a smile at a guy you think you'd like to talk to. Let's all agree on this rule: **Eye contact coupled with a smile means this cab is empty if you'd like to flag it down.** Don't just do the quick eye contact thing that just reads like you think we're coming for your purse. Most men are hesitant to strike up a conversation with a new lady, so we need the encouragement.

I know you think you smile at guys all the time *but you don't*, and it doesn't count if you do it to the backs of our heads. Even if we are married, gay or otherwise, at the very least you've made our day by throwing is one of the delicious smiles we crave. Hell, while you're at it why don't you say, "Now would be a great time to ask me out, you big sissy?" Okay, maybe just the smile for now.

THAT'S JUST YOU LOOKING FOR A LOOPHOLE

I know what you are thinking … If a guy doesn't ask you out but still wants to go hang out that it's probably as good as a date to him, right? WRONG! We can't stress this enough: **guys know that they're supposed to ask girls out**. Otherwise, there wouldn't be four to eight years of proms, homecoming dances, and formal functions that require a verbal invitation, the rental of a tuxedo, and the purchase of a corsage. (Most) Men aren't daft; they're just as ambiguous as women let them be, which actually makes them kind of cunning. If hanging out and hooking up was working for you then you'd be in an awesome relationship, but clearly it's not so here we are. Look, you have to at some point define what it is you deserve in life and then be willing to go get it. If it's dates you want then it's dates you will have, but not by compromising what you *know* feels right to you. A date isn't a marriage proposal, for God's sake; it's a reasonable thing for an awesome chick like you to want. But if you don't put out the vibe that going on actual dates is how someone gets the keys to your kingdom, then dudes are going to keep trying to jump the fence. (Man, we are on a metaphor roll with this book!) For more on first dates, proceed to the next chapter … after you've done the workbook.

CARPE DATEM ROCK'EM SOCK'EM SUPERBOOK

We realize that the idea of having to coerce a guy to ask you out doesn't sit well with everyone and doesn't seem fair. So don't look at it that way. Look at it as you taking control of your life and giving people who obviously don't know what they're missing a fighting chance. Even if it makes you uncomfortable to be so bold or embarrassed to show your cards without seeing theirs, it's the way for you to stack the odds in your favor so that you get asked out more often.

You're only ever going to feel comfortable with the words that YOU are comfortable and capable of saying. So here's your assignment …

Make a list of phrases you can say with the right amount of confidence and flirtation to give a guy the opening to asking you out. We'll start you off with a couple examples of fun and unexpected ways to alert a guy to the awesome opportunity that is you. After that, it's up to you to craft a few gems on your own.

1. "Besides asking me out, what else are you up to this weekend?"

2. "You should ask me out so you at least can tell people you went out with me once."

3. "My friends all said you wouldn't ask me out, but I told them you weren't a pussy."

4.

5.

6.

You get the idea. This is a good exercise whether you use these phrases or not because it forces you to tap into the creative flirtatious and self-possessed sides of your personality. And how is that bad? Oh, it's not.

Thank you, guys.

You are welcome.

BONUS SECTION!
INTERNET DATE-TACULAR!

Tickling the Keypad

Most single people we know have at least dabbled in online dating if not dedicated many of their after hours to the incessant scrolling, clicking and scanning of profiles. If we've been asked it once, we've been asked almost three gazillion times: what are the rules for dating a guy online? Our answer is that it's no different than any other kind of dating. **You have to have the same standards for online as you do in real life.** So if in real life you wouldn't lift your shirt and show everyone your knockers at the bar, then certainly the same should apply online. However, if that is how you roll, then click, click, upload, you wonder bra-wearing superstar! No wonder you have so many "Friends."

HOW TO WRITE A GREAT PROFILE

Like it's not hard enough to answer the three hundred questions and write the sixteen essays that each dating website requires you to complete in order for them to play Cupid and match you up with other people that *also* like to watch TV. You also have to post multiple pictures of yourself so that people can judge how you look at your birthday dinner with friends, what you'd wear hiking with your dog, what you look like on spring break, and that time you met Roger Federer at an airport. People look at your pictures just like you look at theirs and make fun of what you're wearing, check out your body or possibly that other thing that some do when alone and looking at sexy photos. Yes, that's the thing we were talking about and, c'mon, you can't be surprised. We are of the belief that if your profile is specific and creative (creative as in clever, not creative as in totally lying) you'll have a better shot at attracting the kind of person that you could seriously date. Here are our suggestions for making a winning profile.

THE PHOTOS

Everyone looks at your photo first, so let's start with that. We all have that one picture where we photographed better than we ever have in our whole lives. We call that the Gwyneth Paltrow picture. So, your first photo, the one that lures the Internet daters to your profile, should be your Gwyneth Paltrow photo. Your Gwyneth Paltrow photo must be current within the last 2–3 years, must be close to your current weight, and must somewhat resemble you.

The next photo you put up needs to be a personality photo. You playing guitar, you at the beach, you dancing, you doing something that shows what kind of life you live.

The third photo should be your favorite photo of yourself, the one that makes you really happy when you look at it, the one that makes you think all good things about yourself. For instance, you with your family, a candid of you laughing, or you passed out on the floor of the ladies room at TGI Fridays. (*Mini Workbook Pop Quiz: Which of these is a bad choice?*)

Fourth should be a three-quarter to full-body shot because even if you want to hide behind your computer, the goal is to meet in person eventually, so they're going to see it anyway. It's better to be up front with who you are than to go on a date and suffer through the nightmare of some idiot being disappointed by what you look like. (Like he should f***ing judge!)

IMPORTANT NOTE: Look, most people don't like looking at pictures of themselves, but we all recognize when we take a good photo. If that isn't happening for you and you find that when you look at pictures of yourself you're saying, "I don't like my hair"; "I'm too pale"; "I need to lose some weight," seize this opportunity to see what you're putting out into the world and think, "What could I be doing better?" and then start doing something about it. Also make sure you know what's in the background. How you would react if you saw you in a photo wearing a sack dress standing in front of an open can of beans, your Smurf collection, or a week's worth of laundry? No bueno! Imagine the horror of the lady taking a cute photo of herself in the mirror in the bathroom who doesn't happen to notice the floating poop in the unflushed toilet in the background. How many "Epic Fail Selfies" are going to show up on Pinterest or have dedicated Facebook pages? Too many.

CHECKING THE BOXES

Most of filling out a dating profile is checking boxes or clicking a pull-down menu to choose one of the offered selected answers. There's not much we can do for you there except suggest you not be so stringent with your height requirements. Love knows no height, so stop being such a sissy about it. If there's a question that you feel uncomfortable answering then don't answer it, or if that's not an option then pick the preselected answer that makes you laugh the most. It's Just a F***ing Date, so screw them if they can't take a joke! Most of the box-checking categories are pretty easy to navigate, but there's always the tricky one—the "Turn-ons and Turn-offs" or whatever variation of that your site of choice offers. This is where you can attract the creeps, perverts and booty call solicitors. There are always some dumbass options like "erotica" and "skinny-dipping" that, once checked, you will receive a bombardment of winks and emails from people just looking to get cyber-laid. "But what if I love erotica and skinny-dipping?" That's great for you, and you can let your potential suitors know that delicious little tidbit of information about you *LATER ON* after they already like you for all the other great things about you. Erotica, skinny-dipping, photos of you in a bathing suit or anything vaguely naked or sexual will bite you in the ass every time on the Internet. Because regardless of what you're there for, once that card is played, the sexual curiosity of others will trump their desire for dating. Now instead of people responding to your profile and asking you questions about your favorite movies or your work, they'll want to know where you like to skinny-dip or what you're wearing when reading erotica, watching erotica, or getting erotica.

The Headline. Most dating sites give you an opportunity to create a headline that goes with your photo to really sell you to window-shoppers. You get about a hundred to a hundred fifty characters to do this in. Don't use them all. Don't be generic. Do incorporate one specific like or thing that would draw out a person that would connect with you.

Example:

> **Bad Headline:** "Outdoor-loving Midwestern girl looking for someone to share walks on the beach."

> **Why it's bad:** Well, hopefully by your photo they can already tell that you're a girl, and everyone, from the nicest person in the world to a serial killer, likes the beach. Outdoors, again, is pretty general and there are really only a few choices: outdoors, indoors, outer space and underwater, so you're not really narrowing the field with this headline.

> **Good Headline:** "Environmentally conscious and seriously into *The Daily Show*, Cadbury Crème Eggs and Eskimo kisses."

> **Why it's good:** Environmentally conscious tells lookers that you recycle, like organic foods and products, might even drive a hybrid vehicle, and are socially aware, if not active. It also weeds out those that drive Hummers. Seriously into *The Daily Show* reveals that you are probably a liberal Democrat that appreciates satire, enjoys comedy, and keeps up on what's happening in the world though you may not read the newspaper. Cadbury Crème Eggs shows the guy that you have a discerning sweet tooth and you like looking forward to things that come only once a year. Eskimo kisses is the flirtatious part of the headline that is playful but not too sexy. It says that I'll get close enough to nuzzle the right person but I'm not here looking for a booty call.

THE ESSAYS

This is the fun part. This is where you show off your personality, wit and affinities. The fill-in-the-blank questions are usually: "Describe yourself and your perfect date"; "What do you do for fun?"; "Favorite things?"; "Celebrity you most look like." Never answer that last question (or other equally stupid ones); it's a no-win question and your picture is already on your profile, so they know what you look like. Now, about the ones that you should answer: here's what we think. Irony and sarcasm, while very charming (we think), often doesn't read that way, and you can come off pompous or insane when you overuse them in your essays. Don't be afraid to tell people what you are really like, because if you are lucky enough to hit it off with someone, they are going to find out in the long run. You don't want to be going, "Did you think I was serious when I said I liked listening to Carrie Underwood in my Carrie underwear while doing Jell-O shots and preparing my taxes? We're going to have to call the wedding off." You get it? Ironically, by telling everyone who you are not you're missing the opportunity to tell people who you really are. This doesn't mean you can't be funny; just make sure we get some insight as to who you are and what you want. Another popular trick is to act above the dating site, like "I don't usually do things like this." First off, yes you do—we all do. We all seek to meet people and get their approval and there is NO SHAME in it. Meeting online is just as viable as meeting at Skybark (the dog park on the roof of a fancy hotel for people and their pets to meet). Be proud of what you are doing and why you are doing it. Don't act like you've bottomed out and this is your last chance. Don't sound bitter. Yes, dating is hard. Yes, the club scene sucks. And yes, there are a lot of losers out there. But you don't have to remind the people looking at your page 'cause guess what? They are there too and they don't want to be called losers. Everyone is there because it's a cool new way to find folks to date. That's it. Not necessarily to marry or life partner with but just to f***ing date.

Again, like in your headline, it will benefit you to write about things that are specific to you, not about generalizations that are also specific to you.

Example: "Tell us about you."

> **Bad Answer:** "What can I say? I'm a laid-back and easygoing type of person. My friends and family are super important to me and I'd do anything for them. I'm as loyal as they come. I love to laugh and goof around and never take myself too seriously …"

> **Why It's Bad:** This is just information that is way too general because nearly every person on the planet likes to laugh, fancies themselves easygoing, and is close to their friends and family.

> **Good Answer:** "I'm a sunshine girl to say the least. I was born and raised in California, so if it dips below 72 it's sweater weather. Out-of-towners will fight me, but the locals are with me on this one. I have a strong set of beliefs. I believe that *Late Night With David Letterman* is better over coffee (thanks, TiVo); the Hybrid SUV is an oxymoron, but I drive one anyway and love it; there is nothing better than the sound of the ocean; powerful shower pressure can be life affirming (Don't be dirty! I'm talking about the importance of a good shower here.); and a good cup of coffee is imperative to having a good day. I prefer Coffee Bean to Starbucks and I'm not afraid to say it, even if it means being stoned to death one coffee bean at a time. I'm allergic to cats or I just don't like them—I can't remember which one. I like days better than nights, light better than dark, sunny better than overcast, BUT there are few things in this world more magnificent than a really great thunder and lightning storm that kills the power and rocks the house. Mother Nature is a badass! I love a good TV show to rip at the old

heartstrings or tickle the funny bone. Current faves are *Sherlock, Luther, Downton Abbey, Top Gear, Girls, Arrested Development, The Newsroom,* and *Project Runway* (I love watching talented people pursue their dreams.). I am music obsessed and while U2, REM, The Replacements, The Clash and The Pretenders have my teenaged heart, I am currently being rocked by Florence and the Machine, Band of Horses, Buddy, Explosions in the Sky, The XX, Of Monsters and Men, Alex Clare, anything Glen Hansard breathes near, and Wardell. I love a good movie score and think Carter Burwell, Danny Elfman, and Ennio Morricone are masterful; you should check them out if you haven't yet …"

Why It's Good: This essay not only gives you specific information about the things that "speak" to this person but also a sense of their personality. You could more easily sense whether you would be compatible or interested in this profile versus the "bad" one written earlier.

These are our ideas about how to engage the right type of guy online. We hope they're helpful. *However,* we must implore you to try to get in person as soon as possible if you think this thing might have any potential. Even if you're having the loveliest of e-mail or texting relationships, if you finally meet and there's no spark, no chemistry, no physical attraction, it's not going to work no matter how great an e-mail and text writer you or they are. So if you're really cooking by message, take the leap to the phone and then the leap to in person sooner rather than later. It's especially important to meet each other in person before things start going too far to the place of sexual innuendo and suggestion. Why? Because a lot of times once the sexual barrier has been crossed (even if it's only cyber) a few things can go wrong. There's the person that was just looking for a cybersexual relationship, and once they've gotten it they move on to another. You've got the person who, once they've gotten too sexual or too open online, is too embarrassed to meet you in person. Then of course there's the person that thinks that now that you're having cybersex that when they meet you in person it will be to have *actual sex.* That's the super weird thing about Internet or Text Dating: it can go really fast and get really intimate, but then when you finally are with each other in person you don't know if you're on a first date or already a couple, if you're supposed to have your first kiss or already be sleeping together. It's confusing. So be clear and keep it above the waist until you are actually sitting across from each other for conversation.

ESSENCE #3
IT'S JUST A F***ING FIRST DATE!

How to Be a Great First Date and How to Have One

A GOOD DATE IS BETTER THAN GOOD SEX. IT LASTS LONGER AND YOU CAN'T JUST HAVE IT WITH ANYONE.

How's that for motivation to go on dates? Seriously, how great is that?

If used correctly a first date can prove to be an awesome way to get to know a new person, eat some food, take in some art, see a new part of town, and live life like it was supposed to be lived by saying, "What the f***!" and having some fun. Do you see what a great opportunity that is? You can put on an outfit that makes you feel great, spend quality time one-on-one with someone who you have some degree of interest in, and share an experience. IT'S AWESOME … except when it's not. The cold hard truth of the matter is that you're not always going to connect with the person sitting across from you even if you do have *everything* in the world in common. That's why you have to *go and keep going* on dates. There are millions of people out there, and you've got to sort through them somehow to find your match, so why not do it face to face over Mexican food?

There's no one right way to go on a first date, but if you go with the spirit of It's Just a F***ing Date in your heart and mind, though you might not win you're 100% less likely to lose. How do you do that? Just let everything go. Let go of all of your past dating experiences, future hopes and expectations and just *be*.

So let's examine the first date and what it means now to you, the Ultra-Successful Winner Dater type of gal. You shouldn't be overly invested in the guy at this point because after all, you've probably either just met or have a limited knowledge of each other and therefore should have limited or even no expectations. Going into a date without expectations not only lessens the disappointment if it doesn't go well, but more importantly, it increases the possibility for being pleasantly surprised. That's just smart living right there.

So there you are without any expectations getting ready to go on a first date. It's Just a F***ing Date prescribes that you play to win, and that means that even though a first date isn't a big deal you should still be on your game and try. When you honor yourself and the occasion, it not only shows in your appearance but it will radiate out your eyeballs with self-assurance. Imagine the difference you will feel when you begin a first date with the lightness of no expectations, the certainty of his intent, and a shiny new outlook on dating.

What else works on a first date? Be easygoing but don't be easy. Let us not even align ourselves with easy, because we always want to be a challenge. **Easygoing** doesn't mind if we're going for Italian or Chinese. **Easy** doesn't mind if we just stay in and kick it here in your bed.

When in doubt, we're here with a few first date Do's and Don'ts to get you off on the right stiletto.

DEFINITELY DO'S

> **Do be ready on time!** Being late is a great way to tell people that their time isn't as valuable as yours. That doesn't mean you need to be sitting outside the front door waiting for him, but it also doesn't mean he gets to spend forty minutes with your roommate Marla.

> **Do flirt!** Look, if you like a guy then flirt a little and let him know you're having a good time. Flirting comes in a variety of packages. Everything from good-natured ribbing about his basketball team to opening the restaurant door for him. Any version

of actions and words that convey the message "I'm a playful person with a sense of humor, and I'm liking you" will do.

Do eat an actual meal! Be on the date. He picked the restaurant because he likes the food. See if he's got good taste. Hell, if it doesn't work out at least you know another great place to eat with your next date. C'mon, you know you're hungry.

Do compliment him on his choice of restaurant, shirt, or good sense to ask you out. Give the kid props. Planning a date is stressful. Plus, there are a lot of guys that don't like to date, so this guy should be applauded for at the very least knowing you were worth asking out.

DO LET HIM KNOW THAT YOU HAD A GREAT TIME (especially if you want him to ask you out again!). "I had a really good time" is fine. "Those were really good cheeseburgers" is not. "That was fun, we should do this again" is great.

SERIOUSLY DON'TS

Don't drink too much. If we have to explain this one to you then perhaps you might be looking for a different book.

Don't talk about your ex-boyfriends too much. Yes, it's fun to crucify old lovers, but not tonight. Let him find out why people have wanted to date you in the first place (because you're awesome), not why you spent a night in county (you set your ex's clothes on fire when you caught him making out with your roommate Marla. *See*: why you never keep a man waiting.)

Don't ask inappropriate questions. How much money do you make? Have you ever slept with a man? How many women have you had sex with? Zip it, Miss Nosey Pants! It's none of your business and won't be for some time.

Don't go back to their place. I'm sure the movie *Knocked Up* looks amazing in HD, but tell him you'd like to see a movie in a theatre first before checking out his wide-screen.

Don't have sex or get past first base. Do we have to go over this? Most guys who like a girl are only hoping for a kiss. They'll take more if you offer it, but a kiss will do.

FIRST DATE FODDER, BY AMIIRA

Here are the top five questions our babysitters ask me:

1. What should I order? Is it okay to order an appetizer and a main course or is that too much? If he picked the restaurant then he's aware of the prices and the menu and has most likely come prepared. Don't go buffet style hog wild but order what you will eat and don't sweat it. You can always ask what he's thinking about ordering to see if he's going to rock an appetizer, then make the call. Or ask if he'd share a dessert with you later if you skip a salad upfront.

2. Who Pays? He does. He asked so he pays. Should you reach for your wallet and pretend to pay? Not on the first date. The only exception is if he's really sweating over the check, you can offer to split it, but only if you think he's in over his head. You don't want to embarrass him.

3. Should I meet him there? Only if you don't want him to know where you live or are unsure of your ability to leave him *outside* the front door instead of *inside* your bedroom at the end of the evening. Know your boundaries and play it safe.

4. How do I recover from an embarrassing moment on the date? It's all about having a sense of humor and maintaining your confidence. Spill wine down your dress? Offer him the choice of switching outfits or swinging by your house so you can change before the next event. Did you get to the bathroom and realize you had black pepper in your teeth for the entire meal? March back out and throw your napkin playfully at him and tell him that he better beware because you're going get even with him for not being a friend and telling you. Everyone has embarrassing moments, but how you deal with them determines their severity and his impression. If you let them go and find the humor in them instead of being your downfall, it'll be another thing he likes about you.

5. How physical do you have to get on the first date to get asked on a second date? Anything more than a hug and a kiss on the cheek is a bonus. Anything more than a upright make-out session and it can get wonky; too much too soon makes it less valuable. Gauge what you think you want to do and reel it back a step. Guys are hoping for a kiss goodnight. Truly. On a hang out they're hoping for sex, but on a proper date they're hoping you leave them wanting more. Anticipation rules, so don't wreck the opportunity to let him think about you.

TOO MUCH INFORMATION

There's "getting to know you" conversation and there's "please make it stop" conversation. It's important to be able to tell the difference.

Greg's Firsthand Account: There was this girl named Julie who I met while doing stand-up. She had rocking short dark hair and a great laugh. I asked her out and took her to a really cool old-school Mexican restaurant. I noticed right off the bat that she was a little nervous because she talked incessantly, which was kind of cute at first. But then she crossed into no-man's-land when she proceeded to give the details of her sister's recent labor and childbirth, including graphic descriptions of her kin's swollen vagina and pooping on the table, which is apparently a common side effect of childbirth. Now, childbirth is sort of a dicey first date topic anyway, but pooping is a straight up "NO

THANK YOU," at least before the entrée. But more than the content of the story was the complete disregard for the listener. She wasn't noticing, or perhaps didn't care about, my reaction, and the more she talked about her family the more enraged she became, and by the end of the date I wanted nothing to do with her or her family. Even if she had just given the details of the childbirth she should have said something along the lines of: "This is kind of gross; do you want to hear it before eating?" OR "I have a great story to tell you ten dates from now when I know you better and oh, by the way, you should know I hate my family." The moral there would be: think about the kind of images you are putting into your date's head and decide what effect it might have on his chorizo quesadilla.

LEAVE THE ROOM EARLY

Leaving the room early is the term we use for leaving him still wanting more instead of satisfied or sick of you. We've been to a lot of concerts and rarely have they ended too early, but man have some of them gone on too long. Some of them even forced us to go home early and reconsider our relationship with the band.

The philosophy of leaving the room early means when things are going their best, get out. The best way to ensure a second date is leaving the first one on a high note. So if dinner's been a blast, the show was even better, and you're headed home and he asks if you want to stop for coffee, the answer is NO. Even if it's really yes on the inside, NO says I've got things to do in the morning because my life doesn't stop for just anyone. NO says, even though you want to spend more time with me, you'll have to wait. NO says he's going to be thinking about you because he didn't get enough.

The problem with first dates isn't generally the dates themselves but actually all of the shit we pile on top of them. We have all of our past dating disappointments, our nervous energy, the expectations that it's going to suck, the expectations that

DATING ALERT

YOU HAVE TO GET RID OF THE OLD FEELINGS YOU HAVE ABOUT FIRST DATES

The majority of people hate first dates for two reasons. One, because they've been on bad ones and every bad or uncomfortable memory resurfaces every time you're about to give someone else a shot with a first date. Two, because they put too much pressure on the situation instead of just going on it with the attitude of It's Just a F***ing Date! and see what happens. The first date nerves seem to make you momentarily forget that the person they're going out with isn't any of your exes or past bad dates, yet you dump all of your baggage on them before they've even rung the doorbell. Surely they're thinking the same thing about you too, that you're just like their psycho ex-girlfriend or will suffer from at least one, if not all, bad characteristics that belong to her or the last total first date disaster they went on. You have to let it all go, every past dating nightmare and disappointment, and try to recognize that this is a new person that deserves a clean slate and a chance. If you're lucky they'll be smart enough to grant you the same luxury.

you're going to marry this person, the pressure of any of those expectations on both you and them, your insecurities; those head trips we play on ourselves and all the unknown "what ifs" are enough to sabotage any budding interest. It's crazy what we do to ourselves when it comes to dating; then, on top of all that, you've got the sexes at work on a date where the male is sizing up his sexual attraction. (When will we have sex? Will it be good? Can I be attracted to this one woman the rest of my life?) At the same time the female is seeing if there's long-term potential to be found. (Could I marry this guy? Does he want children? Does he have his shit together?) That's not to say that every woman going on a date is looking to get married and every guy is just looking to get laid; it's just saying that the sexes have their own inner wirings that massage them in these directions.

But the point of it is that no one is on a date when they're sizing up what's yet to come. You're in the lab trying to predict what the future will be instead of "in the field" on fact-finding mission or discovery voyage, which is what a first date is supposed to be. The short of it is you are so preoccupied that YOU ARE NOT ON A DATE EVEN WHEN YOU ARE ON A DATE! You can't possibly be if you are focusing on the "what ifs" and hypothetical situations and not on your reactions to each other, your compatibility, your chemistry, your value systems, beliefs, morals, taste in music, films and TV shows, political leanings, religion, favorite foods, sports franchises, hobbies, family values, future plans, etcetera, so on and so forth.

A first date will either be every bad thing you think, a surprisingly good time, or most likely—something in the middle. Now you know. Since you are no longer heading up the Hanging Out and Hooking Up Society, all dates are good dates in one way or another. Every date is an opportunity to practice *going* on a date so that when you meet the right person, you won't blow it by being a terrible date. It's great to go through the exercise even if it's just so you know that you liked what you were wearing, hated that restaurant, discovered that Indian food comes back up on you, and that the story about your uncle wanting to play hide-and-seek with you even in your twenties is better debuted on a later date. It's all just practice so that you can be firing on all cylinders when the time comes.

So let it all go. Start fresh and Carpe Datem.

THE NEW LAWS OF ATTRACTION, BY GREG

Not having an expectation is the new black. This is not to be confused with not caring. You must care that you are on a date, but you must not care where it's all going. That will read loud and clear, and the guy on the date with you will be psyched. I'll let you in on a little secret. Most guys who ask you out will be nervous about it and at some point in the day will have considered calling the whole thing off. I know I felt like that about almost every date I ever initiated. Putting yourself out there with a complete stranger can be a stomach-churning experience. So knowing that your potential suitor feels that way should put you not only at ease but also at an advantage. You can set the tone by letting him know that tonight you are in his hands and whatever he has planned will be great. That may not be the case, but you have a better shot of having a great time by putting the dude at ease. Don't have an expectation, and if he says he's nervous you can remind him that *It's Just a F***ing Date!* In fact, if you both know that going in, you may have the best date ever.

THAT'S JUST YOU LOOKING FOR A LOOPHOLE

Sorry, kitten, but there is no loophole here. You are going on a first date and that's it! Someone has asked for the pleasure of your company and by God they are going to have it. You will not bail on this at the last minute, resort to old patterns or set yourself up for disappointment. That's an amateur move. In fact, you will suit up, show up, and be sparkly and exotic because that's what you should do *all the time in every aspect of life.* You know what else? You will, against all odds, have a great time because as you know, wherever you go is going to be great because you are there! The road to greatness starts on the first date. Got it?

CARPE DATEM ROCK'EM SOCK'EM SUPERBOOK

When a first date comes your way, you need to be ready for it. Whether you do the asking or get asked, it will behoove you to have some solid "go-to" things in place so that you're ready for a rocking date.

FIRST DATE GO-TOS

Put together an outfit for each occasion that makes you **FEEL** attractive and confident. List the pieces from head to toe.

Going for a walk/hike

Having brunch/coffee at a hip café

Going out to a casual dinner and the movies

Going to an expensive dinner

Day at the beach

Fancy event for work

Fancy event for fun

Game night at their friend's

Make a list of restaurants, places you'd like to go, or things you'd like to do on a first date that fall within the budgets below.

Costs less than $10

Costs less than $50

Costs less than $100

Is free

ESSENCE #4
FIRST DATE FOLLOW-UP

Communication and the Next Right Move

The first date is either a beginning or an ending, but what happens next? Unless you drank too much, you can usually tell while you're still on the date how it went, right? WRONG. You only know how it felt for you and how it went for you. What happened on their end, what their impression of the same event is might be totally different than yours. It happens all the time. This is where much of the frustration of dating lies. Two people on the same date with completely different stories—one of them thinks it was great, you totally clicked and can't wait to do it again; the other thinks it was okay but is on the fence as to whether or not they want to see the sequel. Even if you kissed, you never really know how it went, but the thing is that you want to know! That's what this chapter is all about. In the absence of information, what is the next right move?

You are going to hate this, but the next right move is to remain completely still. Not actually still; that would be weird, especially if you have a roommate. They won't understand why you are standing frozen stiff in the kitchen. Even though surely you followed through with our **First Date "Definitely Do's"** from the previous chapter, which included letting your date know what a really good time you had, you will have the urge to call him and reiterate what a great time you had or some version of that. While that's a nice idea, let's be real … you aren't doing it to show him how well versed in the rules of etiquette you are; you just want to find out if he felt the same way. Hate to break it to you, peaches, but that's a classic form of rushing him into a response. So put down the smartphone and just savor the date for a while and *let him do the same*. There is something kind of magical in those first twenty-four hours following a great date where you get to relive moments of it in your head, so enjoy them. In fact, go the opposite direction with your energy. Call your buddies and have a brunch, go for a run to remind yourself that no matter how your heart feels or that your stomach is filled with bees that you are still you, and as such you must take care of you. Don't wait by that phone; in fact, if you can leave yours at home when you go out, then do. Chances are if he had as good a time as you did he's wondering what to do next. Let's let him wonder!

Most guys aren't expecting you to make the next move, and often when you do it backfires. One of the things we have noticed in American culture is an inability to really seduce one another. In our Burger King drive-thru society we like to get to the meal before we get home, barely remembering what the food tastes like. That's because we know we'll eat again. But if we ate every meal like it was our last, we'd spend more time savoring the flavors. That's all we're asking you to do: slow the process down, enjoy it while it's happening, and let it unfold the way it naturally wants to.

If the first date was totally a nonevent, you didn't connect, had nothing to talk about and no chemistry then it's pretty clear that not only won't there be a repeat performance but that it's likely curtains for any further contact. But if there was a spark, an attraction or a connection, then you're now in the waiting purgatory. Was it good for him? Does he like me? Is he going to call? When will he call? How many days is an okay amount of days? How many is too many days? Do I have any messages? Is my phone working? Maybe I should check my e-mail?

Look, a guy knows before the end of the first date with you whether or not he wants to go out with you again. How he plays it if he does want to date you again is what you're waiting to find out. Is he a wait three days caller? A next day texter? Or a disappear off the face of the earth guy? You'll find out soon enough.

Even though you approached your date with a Zen mindset and the It's Just a F***ing Date! attitude, it's not always the easiest thing to carry over after actually having a good date. So don't let your mind run away with you now. Take a moment to recognize that, yes, it would be great if he called, but if he doesn't then it's no biggie. If he wasn't down with the Sparkly and Exotic program that is you for date number two, then he certainly wasn't Mr. Right, Mr. Right Now, or Mr. Knock Your Socks Off In Bed. It's no one's loss but his. Deep breath in, exhale out. Let it go. Okay, good. Now any time you feel yourself getting fixated or anxious about the post–first date contact void just repeat the mantra: "It's just a f***ing date, so let it go." Then take a moment to remember that there are great things in store for all of us and they are all beyond our control. We can't make things happen, but we CAN stop them from happening by screwing things up.

WHAT DOES IT MEAN & WHAT DO YOU DO?

While you're obsessing over his contact, lack of contact or methods of contact, we thought we'd help you decipher what is more than likely happening over at Dude Headquarters and what your response to it should be. While our gut reaction is "Who cares what the hell is going on over there, you're where the action is!" here are some popular scenarios …

	What does it mean…	What do you do?
He doesn't call the next day.	It probably doesn't mean anything. He's probably trying to figure out what his next move is and taking some space to think about you, whether he likes you "that way," and giving you space to do the same	Barely notice because you have plans and aren't expecting to hear from him yet anyway.

	What does it mean...	What do you do?
He doesn't call after two days.	He's doing the regular guy stuff that guys do and either he's considering when the right time to call is OR he's decided not to call.	Continue having your life and DO NOT call, text or e-mail him.
He doesn't call within the first week.	It's not good news. If he likes you and wants to date you again, there will be contact within the first week … barring his deployment to Iraq, his sudden slip into a coma, or the spotty mobile service atop Mt. Everest.	If you like him then you can be sad for a moment, maybe even call a friend to commiserate, then you *let it go*. It was just a date. Move on to the next one.
He doesn't call within the first week, but texts or e-mails, "What have you been up to?"	That means he almost wants to date you and would be open to a booty call.	Don't respond. Seriously. If he decides he wants to see you again he knows where to CALL you. With his actual voice. Like a f***ing gentleman.
He doesn't call within the first week, but texts or e-mails, "Had a great time. Been thinking about you. You free on Friday night?"	That means he almost wants to date you.	Wait awhile to get back to him, then text him that he'll have to call you for the answer.
He doesn't call for three weeks then texts or e-mails, "What have you been up to?"	That means he's looking for a booty call and hoping you weren't crushed enough by him blowing you off to put out.	Wait awhile then text back, "Just dating losers like you."
He doesn't call for three weeks then texts or e-mails, "Been out of town and thinking about you. You free on Friday night?"	That means that the other girl he was dating didn't pan out so he's willing to give it another try with you. Also, that he didn't miss you enough to call you.	Wait awhile then text or e-mail him back, "You must have the wrong number. My name is Mike, but I'm free Friday night."

CONVERTING THE TEXT, BY AMIIRA

Boys will be boys and therefore will often try to get away with the least amount of effort, commitment or communication possible. In our society, the norms are that guys are "bad communicators" and women expect too much from them in this area. Now, because of this stigma, guys think that any form of communication is good enough, should count, and we ladies agree with that ... to a point. Yes, there's the convenience of text messaging or Snapchatting, and there's something sexy about it when you get a "I'm in a meeting but I'm thinking about you. Talk to you later." Sure. But that's because there's a "talk to you later" chaser at the end. When you're in the stages of Post–First Date Meltdown and the phone isn't ringing, texting ain't gonna cut it. **Texting says I'm kind of into you, but calling says I want to hear your voice.** Someone who only text messages you is just keeping you on the line in case he doesn't find someone he's more attracted to by the time he wants to get laid. If a guy's really interested in getting to know you, then contacting you via text, e-mail, IM, social network comment or whatever other modern and impersonal way the geniuses develop next would be SECONDARY to talking to or seeing you in person. HOWEVER, he still might see if he can get away with "shortcut dating" by way of technology in the beginning. It's up to you to be clear that getting to know the glory of you takes place on the phone or in person. *The more you engage in impersonal communication, the more you're going to get it.* The more casual ways of communicating are fine to *supplement* the already existing relationship, but to build one from scratch requires more time than it takes to type Prince-style shorthand into your mobile phone. (U R so funny C U L 8 R.)

How do you convert a texter or an e-mailer into a caller? Simple. Don't accept the idea that his chosen form of communication is enough. When he texts or emails you instead of calling you, then you simply reply with any version of the following:

"E-mail system is being shut down. Call me in
     5 minutes."

"Can't talk now. Call me at 7:00 p.m. Lots to tell you."

"Getting carpal tunnel from texting. Call me on
     my mobile."

"I'm better on the phone. Call me later."

"Typing is my day job. Give me a call."

"I can't remember what your voice sounds like."

You get the picture. Then when he calls, let him know that you're not much of an e-mailer or texter but are awesome on the phone. Basically, if you don't engage in texting and e-mailing instead of talking to each other, he'll have only two choices: to call you or find someone willing to settle for less. For my money, there's nothing like that good night call at the end of the day from the new person you like, and a text just isn't the same.

THE NEW LAWS OF ATTRACTION, BY GREG

Let him call you after the first date.

Just let it lay. Wouldn't you want your date to stand as the last good thing in his mind? Rather than a series of: "Uh, hi. I can't remember if I was supposed to call you, or were you supposed to call me. Anyhooooozle, I just wanted to tell you I had a great time … again. Okay, bye." "Oh, hey, it's me, my phone cut out I think. I just wanted to say, um … had a great time. Okay, bye for now." "Hey, it's me again Janet … from Friday. I forgot to leave my number, it's …" You get the point. If you went out and gave him the best version of you, that's really all you can do. He's had a taste of your delicious company; don't crap on it. Do not replace the awesome lingering thoughts with a shit sandwich. Look, sometimes a dude needs to take a moment to think about what has happened. A guy can like you and want to go out with you again, but want to wait a few days to call you. That's the space he wants to think about you, enjoy thinking about the date, talk to his friends about it and give you plenty of time to do the same while hoping he's going to call. The immediate space is good. It can be delicate too. If you crowd a guy with too many texts, emails, messages, whatever, *it can actually make us like you less*. It goes back to rushing people into doing something they weren't going to do yet and freaking people out with your need to know what they're thinking. Rarely do you know after a first date that it's going to be true love, so we're sitting on a fence after date number one. The fence itself is *liking you*, and on one side is *I really like her/ could love her in the future* and the other side is *NOPE!* You can actually swing us over to the NOPE side.

THAT'S JUST YOU LOOKING FOR A LOOPHOLE

We hear it all the time: it's been two days since your date and you haven't heard from him, but there's been some glitch in your e-mail, voicemail, mobile phone, SIM card or whatever. So you think you should use that as the excuse to make contact. Look, headstrong lady, you can do what you want, but before you do, think about this. If you wanted to reach someone and their gadget had a glitch that disabled it from taking your message, would you stop trying to reach them, or would you find another way? You'd find another way. Now, is this guy who hasn't called you yet a moron? Then let him figure it out. You might find this hard to believe, but YOU'RE WORTH TRACKING DOWN.

CARPE DATEM ROCK'EM SOCK'EM SUPERBOOK

Okay, you are going to hate this, but let us tell you why it's a good idea before you shut us down. We think you should keep a dating journal. "You guys you have to be kidding me." No, we are not. Look, you are now a person who goes on dates. How hard would it be to jot down a couple of notes about the date to remind yourself of who you dated, what you wore, where you went, and what the highlights were? But more importantly, what you did or said that was great, what you did or said that was stupid, did you get kissed, drink too much, etc. ... That way you can go back and see that "Oh man, I loved that blue dress but I hated Crabs A Lot Seafood Playroom." Below is a sample of the kinds of things that are good to remember.

Who did you go out with?

Did you like him?

Do you want to see him again?

Did you make plans to do so or at least tell him, "I had a really good time"?

Did you like what you wore?

Did you like what he wore?

Did you like what you talked about?

Did you like what he talked about?

Were you sexually attracted to him?

Did he try and kiss you?

How did the date end?

What could you have done better?

What was your best moment?

ESSENCE #5
2ND DATE AND BEYOND

Pacing Your Dates and the Formula for Success

So, he ended the suspense and called for a second date because he obviously has great taste and appreciates the finer things in life like you. *So when is it okay to go on the 2nd date?* We think the second date should take place within one week of the post–first date phone call unless your schedule doesn't allow it or one of you is out of town. Then it should be as soon as you can schedule it for the next possible opening. *How many days in advance should he ask?* We're not sticklers about this, but you don't want to appear too available, so we'd say two days in advance at least. *How long should there be between the first and second date?* Here's where we stand—there should be **at least** two days between the first and second dates so that you can build some anticipation about seeing each other and hopefully have another phone call in between to continue getting to know each other. Anything two weeks past the first date and you run the risk of losing momentum and forgetting what you liked about each other on the first date. The reentry to a second date should be smooth and effortless; that's why you want to keep the distance between dates limited; otherwise, it's like having a first date again.

The second date is where things really gel and impressions get cemented. Where the first date is a feeling it out discovery mission, the second date is where you really click or don't. This is a very important date because it's the date where things start happening on the inside. Either you start getting attached to the person or realize that they might not be for you. Though it's important, there should actually be *less* pressure on it. It should feel a bit easier because there is already some level of familiarity, and hopefully there's even been some communication between dates. It's also the date that can be less date-like (not to be confused with *overly* casual). Generally, your date has done his homework on the first date and has some understanding of who you are, so he'll probably ask you on a date relating to some facet of your personality. Like, if you mentioned hiking, then that's a possibility and a totally acceptable second date. If you mentioned you liked the work of Michael Bay (*Die Hard* among others) he may ask you to an action movie, also a totally acceptable second date. HOWEVER, if he asks if you want to rent a movie and order in pizza at his place … IT IS NOT an acceptable second date. Second date is not the date to get that *casual* yet! Trust us: if this thing is going to the distance, there will plenty of time later to kick it couch style with a movie. Hey, hot pants, let us not go anyplace—yours nor his—with an adjacent bedroom. It's just not time yet. This is still a very crucial point in developing what could be a relationship, and **it's imperative that on date two you leave the room early.**

Here is a quick list of acceptable and unacceptable second dates.

Acceptable:
Dinner out
A movie (It's a classic)
Bowling or mini golf
Dancing
Concert
Hike, bike ride or any outdoor activity
Art museums (Cultural and romantic!)
Coffee.

Not Acceptable:
Lunch (Too early, feels like a downgrade)
Breakfast (Late night after a movie or concert's okay; otherwise, same as above)
His place for a movie

Your place for sex
Drinks (Not time to meet for drinks just yet)
The cafeteria at your dorm (Even if he doesn't
have any money, he can take you to a coffee shop
for tea. Everyone can get five dollars from going
through their pants pockets.)

What about getting frisky? The second date is a fine time to get your smooch on, *but that's it.* Again, we're not saying that sex is anything less than stellar or that you shouldn't get to have it, but WAIT!!! **You can't lose by parceling out the good stuff**, and believe us, your kisses are like Super Bowl tickets—hard to come by and f***ing awesome! Let the little things speak of what the future might hold instead of showing him what's behind door number one before he's even taken a stab at solving the puzzle. Remember: teaser, trailer, THEN movie!

DATING ALERT

While dating someone is great, dating more than one someone is even better. What better way to determine how deep your feelings are for someone than by having something to compare it to? We believe that it's good to date in the classic sense. Look, in the old days before the advent of the Girls Gone Wild generation, people used to date more than one person. See, back then, before premarital sex you dated a bunch of people and then decided whom you wanted to get it on with for the rest of your life, and hopefully it worked out.

It's easy to date lots of people when you are not having sex, but it's hard to marry someone these days and not have had sex since premarital sex is so widely practiced and enjoyed. So why not date lots of people, then find the one you want to have sex with, then use *that* as an indicator that this is the person you are serious about. Another huge upside to dating more than one person is that it takes the pressure off of hoping that this one person will work out, plus it keeps you busy so you don't go too fast. The reason more people don't actively date more than one person is because they get into relationships so quickly. There seems to be a "sex on the third date" model that people are following. Then, because the intimacy of having sex often implies more than "just dating," the next thing they know, date three has become an instant relationship. Unless of course you've both agreed to dating and sleeping with other people as well, which most people don't have the foresight to do before having a naked party. Or maybe you've agreed to sleeping with other people because you're a time traveler who lives in the 1970s. "But do I have to tell my date that I'm dating other people?" Not unless he asks, and all you have to tell him is "I'm dating." For some reason people feel the need to disclose everything right away. Keep some mystery. You don't owe anyone any explanation of how you live your life, especially on a first or second date. Trust us, the more you date, the easier it will be to find the one you like. That's just good math.

Dating is the best system of eliminating people that aren't right for you and finding the one that is. It's the smartest way to move into the land of a serious relationship, because then what you have is built on a mutual attraction (both physical and psychological), emotional attachment and respect for each other. It's a formula that worked for generations and hence is a classic. Get it? Old ideas along with new ideologies about sex: we like to think of it as a Custom Classic for today's Sparkly Super Dater. Now, if you're experiencing a dating drought (which is quite common in this part of the world) and you can't find anyone else to date that's of any interest to you besides bachelor #1, then still take it slow and really evaluate how you feel about this person instead of how you *want* to feel about someone.

After the second date, assuming it went as well as we think it probably did, we loosen up a bit and are less stringent about you calling him. That's not to say that you should do it a lot. The goal is to still *leave him wanting more* and when he wants more, he is still in pursuit, and that's a good thing. When timing out when to go on dates three, four and five, they can get closer together like going out every two days or so, though we still advise to space them *at least* one whole day apart. That means from dinner to dinner the next night, not dinner to breakfast the next morning! No same day dating until date #7. By date six, we're not against you moving the date to your place or his for a home-cooked meal or takeout and a movie, but keep your clothes on and be clear and flirty about it. "I'm inviting you over for a meal. So don't bring pajamas or anything." But keep dating other people until you know for sure that you've found the guy that you want to date exclusively … then you can cut the other fellas from your dating lineup one by one until the genius figures out that you're the one for him too!

THE NEW LAWS OF ATTRACTION, BY GREG

Let him ask you on that second date; after that it's up to you to do what feels right for yourself. If you want to ask him out for date number three, who's to stop you, *but let him chase you down again first*. If things went the way you hoped, he's going to be chomping at the bit to get to see you again. And he should be, because you kick ass. Look, the first date sets the tone for who you are and how you like to be treated; the second date reaffirms that by continuing with the same standards and mindset. He should be hustling to figure out what happens next. It's important to put some space between the first and second date just to continue to build the anticipation, so no same day ask outs. "But Greg, I was free, really." Hopefully you won't be free because of your super busy life *but also because it's not time to show him how easy it is to hook up with you.* That way, when you eventually do break plans for him further into the relationship, it's a big deal. Right now you are a rare and awesome bird that people have to climb a few mountains of disappointment to see.

(Notable exceptions: If your first date was Dec. 30th and he wants to take you out for New Year's that's okay, but you should ALREADY have plans; or if he's got No Doubt reunion tickets, because they can't wait for you. We asked.)

THAT'S JUST YOU LOOKING FOR A LOOPHOLE

But what if I'm not sure if I like him? Do I have to go out with him? Yes, you should. Sometimes we don't click with someone because they're just plain aren't a match for us, but sometimes we don't click with someone because they are not what we are used to dating, which is a totally different thing. Love, just like life, comes in a different package than you expect it to, so give the guy a second shot if you're on the fence. What's another couple of hours with someone who obviously thinks you're great going to hurt? At the very least it will be good for your self-esteem, and at the very best it could also be the date that changes everything. If the guy was a good enough guy and seemed to really put in an effort, despite how nervous he may have been, give the guy a second chance. Why, you ask? Because that's the kind of ultra-successful winner dater you are. In case we haven't told you, one of us wasn't sure if we liked the other, but we went out on a second date anyway to find out, and look where we ended up … getting to write a dating book for you!

CARPE DATEM ROCK'EM SOCK'EM SUPERBOOK

Second date assessment quiz. Not sure if you want to go out on that second date? Here's a quick quiz to put you on one side of the fence or the other.

Question	Point Value	
Did he show up on time?	Yes	+2
	No	-1
Did you like what he was wearing?	Yes	+1
	No	-1
Did you think he was Handsome?	Yes	+2
	No	+1 *(That's right, give his looks another chance because people can become more attractive as you get to know them.)*
Was the conversation easy to make?	Yes	+2
	No	-1
Was the conversation interesting?	Yes	+2
	No	-1
Did he have a good sense of humor?	Yes	+3
	No	-3
Did he get your sense of humor?	Yes	+3
	No	-3
Were you attracted to him?	Yes	+2
	No	-1 *(That can change on date #2.)*
Did he have good manners?	Yes	+2
	No	-2
Was he affectionate?	Yes	+1
	No	-1
Was he too grabby?	Yes	-3 *(We shouldn't have to reward him for not being a creep.)*
	No	+1

Were you more impressed by him than you expected?	Yes	+2
	No	+1 *(No points off for being what you expected him to be.)*
Did he have a plan for the date?	Yes	+2
	No	-2
Did you like what he had planned?	Yes	+2
	No	+1 *(At least he planned something!)*
Did you want him to call after the first date?	Yes	+2
	No	-1
Did you think about him the next day?	Yes	+2
	No	-1

Let's add them up and see how our guy did! If he scored anything above a 20, then by God you're going on that second date. If he scored between 14–20 then you should still go and give it another shot. Anything below 14 and you should pretend he has the wrong number when he calls.

ESSENCE #6
SEXCLUSIVITY

Getting It On and Locking It Down

If you read just one chapter of this book let it be this one because it's about sex and when to have it. As stated earlier in this book, we love sex and like to hear that people are having it. We also think that if you really like someone you should WAIT to have it. We are not advising you wait for some chaste or moral reasons but rather because **you have a much better chance of becoming a couple** if you do. Exclusivity and sex are meant to go together but one (Sex) is not a means to the other (Exclusivity).

Sex has a very prominent place in a good relationship but like any good thing, people have managed to kind of f*** it up. People use sex as a reward or as a bribe; they use withholding sex as a punishment because we as a people have figured out that SEX IS GREAT AND PEOPLE WANT LOTS OF IT! Which is why many use sex as a device to persuade people to rush into relationships that they're not completely ready to commit to. It's certainly a tactic that can work in the *short term* but in the long term it's a crapshoot at best. Remember what we told you about coming along at your own pace? That goes both ways if you want to have a great relationship—the other person has to arrive at their own feelings uncompromised just as do you; otherwise, you have a relationship based on the desire to have sex for the first time. Let's be honest about it: the desire to have sex with someone is a little more common and a lot less lasting than you think. It can compel you to get there, but it can't keep you there.

Just like we encourage you to value yourself, not be too

available, and slow down when you date, we have to stress that those ideals apply tenfold to having sex. Having sex changes things and puts the relationship on a different trajectory. It can rocket you into the exclusivity of coupledom or it can shake you out of any assurance you had about the connection with another person. If one of you had unspoken expectations tied to having sex and the other didn't, you're in trouble. Or if one of you gets freaked out because of what sex means to them, for them, or what they think *you think*, it means you're in trouble. In short, if you're both not equally invested in the outcome of having sex, you can get spanked by it … but not in a hot, sexy way.

We've heard friends say when dating someone new that they "just wanted to get it out of the way." What? Sex, yummy sex, something that we should be anticipating, looking forward to, thinking about, and wanting, you mean that sex? That's the one we should just get out of the way? Would you eat a bowl of cake batter for dessert instead of letting the cake bake, frosting that sucker, and relishing every bite of it? You'd rather have a stomachache and a great sense of regret instead of delicious cake?

Getting it out of the way is a horrible way to look at the first time you have sex with someone new. As though it's a chore like doing the dishes rather than what it should be—which is the ultimate way of sharing yourself with someone and rocking their (and your) world. There really isn't any greater way (other than a mixtape, CD, iTunes playlist) to share your love than sex … except for having sex while listening to the mixtape, then having a cake encore. Sex should matter. If you don't make having sex matter, then it will be of NO VALUE to either of you.

It's our position that you shouldn't be having sex with everyone that you're dating *if* you want a *COMMITTED* relationship. Sex should signify that you're serious about *A* as in *ONE* person. It should have some value, some significance, and if you bestow it with that value and significance, it can be the thing that sets you apart from all the other girls he has dated. It's a traditional idea, but if you want to have a boyfriend you shouldn't have sex with anyone until that status has been cemented. No exceptions.

While we're talking about it, sex shouldn't be the carrot you dangle to get the commitment; it should just be the thing that you only have while in a committed and exclusive relationship. That should be the standard that you live by. That tells the guy you're dating that sex with you is special and that you don't just hand it out as a party favor for any schmo who takes you out on the town.

So then how do you get to be boyfriend/girlfriend without having sex and without using sex as a motivation? Look, sex is always going to be an incentive, but you don't want to be the kind of girl that positions it that way because that's lame and completely beneath an Ultra-Successful Winner Dater like yourself that has standards, a life, self-worth, and is picky about who they choose to spend their valuable time with. Well, under the assumption that you are actively dating (*which for the sake of this we'll define as seeing each other at least once a week and talking on the phone three days a week if not more—in addition to, NOT INSTEAD OF, any extracurricular e-mails, text messages, IMing, and such, if you so partake in those activities*), then it's up to you to first decide *IF* this is the guy for you. Really think about it: How do you feel about ONLY being with him? How do you feel about NOT being with him? If *YOU'VE* decided that he's the one for you, then it's up to you to let him know that you are beginning to feel strongly for him (without having sex with him). You can let him know that you're "thinking" about letting go of the other guys you've been dating and gauge his reaction. He may just tell you right then that he's ready to make things exclusive. If he doesn't jump at the opportunity for exclusivity, then he's probably still on the fence about doing the same. That's what we call good information to have *BEFORE* you have a naked party, don't you think? You don't want to be sharing a guy sexually because that's THE most direct route to insecurity and low self-esteem you can find. So it's simple to say, "Look, I only have sex with people that I'm seeing exclusively. I'm not trying to define this as much as I'm doing what's healthy and smart for me. If this doesn't work for you then that's okay, but these are the standards by which I live my life." Our guess is that he'd be psyched to be included in such a program. It's pretty safe to say that if you are sleeping together and are not seeing others then you are on your way to becoming boyfriend and girlfriend. Obviously, your sexual compatibility will determine if you want to proceed further.

Okay, hot shots, what do we do and how long do we have to wait? We say ten dates or a minimum of three weeks to four weeks of dating. That's right, we've added seven dates, one whole week's worth, to the three-date rule and we strongly feel that it is a reasonable amount of time to wait. Considering that people used to wait until they were married, which is like an eternity, you can "Woman Up" and wait ten dates or three or four weeks. Seriously, it's a blip in the scheme of things, and in the end you will have honored yourself and each other. Even if it doesn't work out, you can at least say you gave it you're best shot and not be wondering if you slept with him too soon.

If you've paced yourself, built a relationship based on an emotional investment, mutual respect, and a healthy dose of anticipation, then sex is going to be even better and more exciting. Why is that? Because there will be an understanding that doing the deed is something that is reserved only for the elite.

Why does sex have to be such a big deal? *BECAUSE IT JUST PLAIN IS!* Answer us this: Why shouldn't it be? Why would they make sex feel so good if it wasn't supposed to be a big deal? What is the value in downgrading its worth or the power it has to not only give you pleasure but to elevate the relationship and make the connection you have more profound? Making sex matter with the person you love is a great thing because there is no more intimate way of sharing yourself. So why not make that a momentous occasion? One that has been planned out, thought about, and worked for. Why not make it mean something? Why not give it value? After all, this guy isn't just having sex with anyone: **HE'S HAVING SEX WITH YOU** and that's a big deal!

We never said don't be sexual or sexy, and again this is not a moral mandate, this a suggested way of getting the best out of your relationship. It is also about drawing out the good stuff, making all the moments count and building to something memorable. So if you aren't supposed to have sex for ten dates or three to four weeks, what can you do? Let's cut to the chase: what counts as sex? Climaxing by either of you counts as sex and therefore should not be done. That means whenever things get steamy YOU STOP! Oral sex counts as sex and should not be done because it also generally leads to climaxing. Heavy petting is okay as you approach the goal line but *not before*. Keep your clothes on, keep your pants up, and enjoy the glory of the journey because it's one of the best ones we get in this lifetime.

We've mapped out a timeline so you can know where to draw the lines.

> **Date 1**: At the very least, if you like this guy, a peck on the cheek and a hug. If it was a particularly good date, *ONE* good passionate kiss. We really don't care who initiates. If you are feeling it go for it. *BUT JUST ONE*. A sampler. Don't turn it into a make out session. Especially if it feels like it could go there. Trust us, he'll be thinking about that kiss all the next day wondering if he'll get more or why he didn't.

> **Date 2:** Well, sister, it appears he enjoyed your ONE kiss last date. Tonight, what's it going to hurt to make out a bit? Really enjoy the kissing because sadly, in relationships, making out is the thing that goes first, which is so sad because making out in the early stages is awesome. So rock a make out party. What about his hands? Keep them above the clothes and off the juicy bits. That goes for your hands too. Really concentrate on the kissing.

> **Dates 3, 4, 5:** We are aware that in many modern relationships these are the dates where people "get sex out of the way." It's almost an industry standard, so it's probably time, if you haven't already started, to have conversations about sex. These conversations can almost be as exciting as

the act itself. Acknowledge that you like sex and that it is something that is important to you, but you don't just have it with anyone, especially if you are dating more than one person. You don't have to tell him how many dates you are waiting or what your time frame is, just that it's NOT time. Keep him on the make out party plan. If he wants to know what's under that shirt of yours, that's up to you, but KEEP YOUR PANTS ON … for now.

Dates 6, 7: Here's something we know for sure. Men love great underwear. Perhaps it's time for an underwear make out party with above the waist action. Know when to stop because it's not time for the "Happy Ending," if you know what we mean. That's not until game day!

Dates 8, 9: Bring on the heavy petting and NO SEX SLEEPOVER party. While you can pet away there should be **NO CLIMAXING!!** Mouth can do some exploring and pleasure seeking, but it stays above the belt. The mouth counts as sex, and climaxing messes with guys' heads and therefore is considered SEX. *SEX*—not messing around sexy foreplay. Comprende??

Date 10: Ta-da! You have waited for the big event and worked each other up into a frothy lather, so tonight should be memorable to say the least. Be safe, use protection, and have fun!

CASUAL SEX CLAUSE, BY GREG

I worked on *Sex and the City* for three years, so I am more than aware that women, like men, like to have sex for sport. Trust me, we fellas are all for it, just as long as that's *REALLY* what you want. No doubt there are days where you just want to get laid. Why not? Sex is a great part of life. But make sure you're being honest with yourself about why you are doing it. Don't lie to yourself that you are okay with something casual if in fact you want something more serious. It's okay to want more; just don't try and come in through the back door (not that back door!) and gamble that he'll develop the feelings you want him to. More often than not, one of the two people having a casual sex relationship develops deeper feelings and attachments and the other doesn't. Have casual sexual relationships turned into something more? I'm sure it's happened, but more often than not we are asked, "How can I turn my booty call into a boyfriend," and to that we usually throw our hands up and say, "Turn back time and don't be a booty call in the first place." When I was dating, there were girls I went out with and girls I called at 4:00 a.m. … AND THEY JUST WEREN'T THE SAME GIRL. I also had a crush on a girl who only wanted sex. I kept hoping I could turn it into a relationship but I never did. So make sure you are honest with yourself and the person you are having sex with about what it is. They may want more from the situation than you do, in which case full disclosure is a must to avoid hurt feelings. Be safe and rock the sheets, and when you're ready to settle down, close up shop until you find the right customer.

THE NEW LAWS OF ATTRACTION, BY GREG

You are worth the wait. How many more ways can I say it? I took an informal poll of the Internet and here is what I found out. 97.9% of the men surveyed said that if they were dating Emma Stone they would gladly wait ten dates to have sex with her. I know what you are saying. "Well, I'm not Emma Stone." Okay, fair enough, but that's not the point. The point is that if Emma Stone held herself to a ten-date policy these men would respect that. It's about a value system. Amiira and I waited. She is my Emma Stone. If I like you enough to respect you, I'll wait because you have told me by virtue of the way you carry yourself a half for business meetings, but because we worked on projects together we spoke daily. After a while it became clear that he was coming to our office more frequently and working out of my office specifically instead of the conference room that he normally used. Then one day he called me and asked, if he flew into town, would I have dinner with him? I was certainly flattered that he thought a date with me was worth the hassle of air travel, and we did get along really well, so I agreed and up to New York he flew. We had a great date, flirted shamelessly, shared some kisses, and agreed that we should do it again. So the next week he flew up, we had a great date with flirting and kissing, and started talking every day on the phone. Same thing for week three—flew up, dinner, flirting, making out (this time IN my apartment, not at the front door), then off he went and we talked every night on the phone before we went to sleep. By week four and our fourth official date, I was feeling pretty excited about this guy and hopeful again about the possibility of getting back on the horse so quickly in a world where all my friends had told me that dating sucks. (*Not for me, pal!*) Our situation seemed almost perfect so far. We had known each other for a couple of years, worked together well, had been kind of dating for a month, were definitely attracted to each other, and he made a huge effort to see me because flying to New York every week cost time and money. Not to mention that I wasn't really ready for a full-time relationship yet, so his living in another city was good for now. So we're on the fourth date and I'm seriously considering having sex with this guy tonight. It's been a month that we've been dating, it seems like we're going somewhere with this thing, and I think I'm ready.

So we have "THE CONVERSATION." You know the one. The "are you sleeping with anyone else?" conversation that you always have before you jump in the sack with someone who you're considering getting into a relationship with. That one went pretty well. Neither of us was currently sleeping with anyone else. Then we had "THE OTHER CONVERSATION," which always follows the first CONVERSATION and starts with: "How many people have you slept with?" He said, "You first," to which I smugly replied, "Six." I'm not going to lie: I was feeling pretty proud of how low my number was. Sure, I had been in a relationship for the last five years, so obviously I had been out of the game, and yes, I did get married at the foolishly young age of twenty-three (which was pre-cell phones and Internet BTW, so dating was actually still dating, not this bullshit you people made up in the last ten years). So clearly I had been resting on my SIX for a while. "What about you?" I asked the new dreamy guy that I was making future sex plans with in my head. And I shit you not, this is VERBATIM what he said to me: "Including my brother's wife or not?" Now, it took me a second to digest the information in his words because he asked it so matter-of-factly, as though he had said, "Is today Tuesday?" And he definitely was NOT kidding! So I smiled and tried to keep my expression from showing any alarm or judgment and asked him, "Well, why wouldn't you count her?" And again, I shit you not, this is what he said: "Because I didn't come." Needless to say, I didn't have sex with this person nor did I ever go out with him again, but we did continue to work together, which was a little weird because I knew he had sex with his brother's wife. Had I already had sex with him before having this mind-blowing character-defining piece of information, I WOULD HAVE BEEN THROWING UP IN MY MOUTH at the dinner table. Waiting to have sex paid off big for me, and I'm grateful that I had the sense to take it slow because otherwise I'd probably still feel yucky about having sex with "that" guy.

CARPE DATEM ROCK'EM SOCK'EM SUPERBOOK

For those of you who will have a hard time waiting to have sex, it's time for the great ways to postpone sex workbook exercise. Come up with ten ways to keep having sex at bay. We'll start you off with a couple, but it's up to you to not only think of more but to actually do them and keep your knickers on!

WAYS TO POSTPONE SEX, BY (INSERT YOUR NAME HERE)

1. Don't go to their house or your own for dates.

2. Strip your bed before he comes over and throw your sheets in the washing machine so that they're wet and the bed isn't inviting.

3. Paint a bedroom wall so that the fumes keep the bedroom off-limits.

4.

5.

6.

7.

8.

9.

10.

A FEW WORDS BEFORE YOU TAKE THE FIELD

Dearest You,

We have great hope for you finding happiness. Let us leave you with a couple more thoughts before you head out into the world as a Super Extraordinary Ultra-Successful Winner Dater.

YOU BOYZ 'N' BOOZE!

You won't get a lecture from us on the evils of drinking and dating; we are sure you know the score on that one. We just have one simple rule. **Don't drink anything, smoke anything, or take anything that makes you a different person or makes you make different decisions than you would were you sober.** Look, you've spent all this time becoming an even better you, so don't ruin all that hard work by becoming "Miss Boozy Forgets Her Standards" if that's what too many Guava Gin Tumblers does to you. Pace yourself because in the end it's **YOU** he wants to know, not the girl that lifts her skirt over her head. (Sure, he'll have sex with the girl who pulls her skirt over her head, but he won't take her home to mom.)

EAGER IS FOR BEAVERS.

Here's another gem of wisdom for you … Don't make yourself too available or be too eager. Do not stop your already fulfilling life at the drop of the hat. When you bail on your life and friends for a new person, the message you're sending that new person is: *"My life isn't that great and I'm going to be needy because I'm putting all my eggs in your basket."* It's the honest to God truth. For every action there is a consequence, and even the ones you think aren't a big deal can have seismic repercussions.

You being so excited that you spend every second with them = you being too available.

You being too available = them feeling too responsible for you.

Them feeling too responsible for you = you being needy.

Even if you didn't mean for your actions to provoke that train of thought, it most likely will, because it's hard to manage feelings and expectations on both ends.

ZIP IT!

Our feeling when you're dating someone new is that a little goes a long way. Don't reveal everything too fast. Parcel out the good stuff and let them relish all the interesting bits, pieces and facets of the superstar you are. Keep some thoughts to yourself (*for the time being*) and let him think and wonder about you. People should earn the things you share with them based on their interest and emotional investment in you. You don't need to give your biography on the first date and you don't have to solve the "what kind of underwear is she wearing?" mystery either. No one needs to know everything about you or *GETS* to know everything about you. If you're dating a quality person that the opportunity exists for a future with, then you'll have plenty of time to compare every experience, heartbreak or desire you've had in life as well as favorite sexual positions. Hell, we've been together for nearly a decade and we still learn new things about each other. So zip it, why don'tcha!

CARPE DATEM!

Love,
Greg & Amiira

CPSIA information can be obtained at www.ICGtesting.com
Printed in the USA
BVOW02s1647241214

380822BV00005B/220/P